To the Students of Alberta

This book is dedicated to those who will shape the future character of Alberta. It is written in the expectation that Alberta students are very directly interested in the people and conditions which shaped their present circumstances. The book was developed by Alberta Education to provide a source of information on the people of our home province. It may also serve as an inspiration to those who will soon be taking responsibilities for this province's future.

The Honourable David King
Minister of Education

The Albertans

Lone Pine Publishing

The Albertans

Written by:
> Ken Bolton
> Sharon A. Fogarty
> Donaleen Saul
> Sheonaid Ursan

Research by:
> Jean Crozier
> R.R. Kennedy
> Elaine Trimble

Edited by:
> Grant H. Kennedy
> James B. Stanton

The Publishers

Lone Pine Media Productions Ltd.
#403 10189 - 101 St.,
Edmonton, Alberta.

Printed and bound in Canada
by Bulletin-Commercial Printing Ltd.
14425 - 118 Ave., Edmonton.

Typesetting and design by
Horizon Line Typecraft Ltd.
17220 - 107 Ave., Edmonton.

Canadian Cataloguing in Publication Data

Main entry under title:

The Albertans

    Bibliography:P.176

    Includes index

    ISBN 0-919433-00-6

29,710

    1. Alberta - Biography.
I. Bolton, Ken, 1943-   II. Kennedy, Grant
H. [Grant Hugh], 1935-   III. Stanton, James
B., 1939-
FC3655.A42   971.23'009'92   C81-091136-1
F1075.8.A42

Dedicated to:

The Youth of Alberta

in anticipation of their achievements
over the next 75 years

Photo Credits:

Acknowledgements:

The preparation of this book has been made possible by the initiative of the Curriculum Branch of Alberta Education and the direct and enthusiastic support of David King, Alberta's Minister of Education. In addition, the management and employees of Suncor, Inc. contributed to the publication of 15 colour reproductions of paintings by Calgary artist Don Inman. These paintings of prominent Albertans, many of whom are principal subjects of this book, have now been donated to the people of Alberta.

The Albertans was developed by the Alberta Compendium Project Committee as a 75th Anniversary project from Alberta Education. Chairman of the Committee and Director of the Compendium Project was William F. Lockhart of Alberta Education. The members were: Douglas Francis, Department of History, University of Calgary; John Patrick Gillese, Alberta Culture; Terry Kernaghan, Alberta Education; Doug Ledgerwood, Alberta Educational Communications Corporation (ACCESS); Beverley Mitchell, Department of English, University of Alberta; Mary Ricard, Alberta Education; and Kathleen M. Snow, Faculty of Education, University of Calgary. All gave generously of their several and varied talents to make the project a success. Their design of a novel project and selection of 75 names from more than 300 suggested by interested groups and individuals throughout the province was a difficult and unenviable task.

Thank you.

Grant H. Kennedy
James B. Stanton

Table of Contents

Before 1905   p.13

1905 – 1918: As They Sow...   p.16

A.C. Rutherford   Tom Three Persons
Frank Oliver   Stephan G. Stephanson
The Grey Nuns   A.W. Dingman
Henry Marshall Tory   J.B. Collip
A.E. Cross   Emily Murphy
Bob Edwards   William Pearce
William Fairfield   William Griesbach

1919 – 1929: A New Furrow   p.43

Henry Wise Wood   Roland Gissing
Fred Brewster   Herman Trelle
Irene Parlby   Jimmy Simpson
Nellie McClung   W.R. "Wop" May
Karl Clark   Louise McKinney
J. Percy Page

1930 – 1938: The Lean Years   p.63

R.B. Bennett   William Aberhart
Pat Burns   Charles Sherwood Noble
William Irvine   Leonard W. Brockington
Elizabeth Sterling Haynes Georges Bugnet
J.W. Barnett

1939 – 1947: Abroad and Home   p. 81

George Pearkes   Matthew Halton
Wilf Carter   Chester Ronning
Grant McConachie   Alexander Calhoun
Hedwig Bartling   Illingworth Kerr
Donald Cameron

1948 – 1960: The Bumper Crop   p.113

W.G. Hardy
Clifford E. Lee
Laura Attrux
Mary Percy Jackson
Earle Parkhill Scarlett
Raymond Urgel Lemieux
William H. Swift

Eric L. Harvie
W.O. Mitchell
Walter Campbell MacKenzie
James Gladstone
Maxwell Bates
Frank McMahon

1961 – 1970: A Changing Harvest   p.137

Al Oeming
Violet Archer
Max Bell
Andy Russell
John Decore

Grant MacEwan
Roland Michener
Ernest C. Manning
Mel Hurtig

1971 – 1980: ...So Shall They Reap   p.153

Peter Lougheed
Timothy Byrne
Max Ward
Maria Campbell
Joseph Schoctor

John P. Gallagher
Ralph Steinhauer
Tommy Banks
Don Smith
Joe Clark

INDEX   p. 170
REFERENCES AND SUGGESTED READING   p.176

Before 1905

by John Patrick Gillese

Just over 110 years ago, the wife of Methodist minister George McDougall watched with eyes that could weep no more as her husband and one son, David, buried her two daughters and another son's wife (all victims of a smallpox epidemic) in the mission graveyard at Pakan, 70 miles downriver from Fort Edmonton.

"It is a hard thing," her son said, as they filled in the earth, "to bury our own dead."

It was part of the price paid to open up the West.

Hardship, loneliness, danger were no strangers to the first Albertans.

Not to Peter Pond, caulking his canoes with tarry sand where Fort McMurray stands today.

Nor to Father Lacombe, dodging Cree and Blackfoot bullets 13 years after he had vowed to spend his life to bring peace to "the children of the plains," and whose love for them proved greater than their hate for each other.

Not even to someone like "Slippery Annie," who stars in the colourful folklore of southern Alberta as the woman who finally got her husband-to-be to show up for the wedding — dead drunk. "Bring him back when he's sober!" ordered the appalled clergyman. "The trouble is," poor Annie responded, "he won't come when he's sober."

Few of those who "came West" before Alberta was a province were as colourful as Jerry Potts, the bandy-legged scout for the

13

RNWMP, or John Ware, the famous Black cowboy. But in a less dramatic way they were as rugged and independent as Billy Henry who, at the age of almost 100, was finally induced to enter a Senior Citizens' Home, only to take off the next morning for his cabin near High River. His reason for leaving? "Too danged many old people in that place."

In preparing this book about famous Albertans, some 326 personalities were formally considered: explorers, missionaries, traders, ranchers, farmers, law-makers – (perhaps even a few law-breakers, most of whom led exemplary lives in this province where people could bury their past, could build their own future).

Space, for one thing, precluded the possibility of featuring more than a select few. Additionally, all occupants and all decades of our history had to be represented. Hence, the major portion of this book has been given over to the history of Alberta since its inception as a province – and those who made that history.

Many Alberta pioneers are portrayed in fine paintings by Calgary artist Don Inman: a gift to the people of Alberta by the Suncor Corporation, via the Alberta Art Foundation. The life stories of many more – known and unknown, colourful, or of the steady stuff on which lasting progress is built – remain a rich human historical resource to be researched and written by our authors who, themselves, may be descendents of these pioneers. The point is: every land needs its heroes; and this work is designed to acknowledge the debt we owe to so many, the unnamed as surely as the famed.

In such debt, Alberta is rich. Where explorers and missionaries lit their campfires, our cities stand "golden in the sun" today. The character, the courage, the ideals of those who opened up our West live on today in the excellence and achievements of their children and grandchildren. The interdependence of neighbours – whose unfailing asset was the sure help of one another through good times and bad – brought into being a singularly-united and warm-hearted people whose way of life is the envy of much of the world.

The death of the Rev. George McDougall, in a way, typifies all those, known and unknown, whose lives are touched on in this book – but especially those courageous first settlers who put down roots that have made Albertans strong, proud and independent to the present day.

The elder McDougall died on a buffalo hunt in January, 1876 – when the old West was ending and a new Alberta was soon to be born. Alone, separated from his son, John, and their small hunting party, he knew death was coming in the bitter sub-zero cold,

14

*and he met it as he had met every other challenge of his lifetime. When
Indians found him, his body was laid out as if for burial.*

"His work was finished," said his son at the funeral.

Only in a sense.

In another sense, it had only begun.

*That faith, courage and greatness of heart of all our early settlers
lives on in the way of life that makes Alberta the good land it is today.*

– J.P.G.
February, 1981

1905 - 1918

As They Sow...

The North-West Rebellion was a generation past and rail-roads had transformed the territory. In Edmonton crowds had gathered in the sunshine of an early September morning. Alberta was to be proclaimed a province – the eighth in the Dominion of Canada. A territory had come of age.

A.C. Rutherford

Alberta became a Canadian province on September 1, 1905. The next day, it had the only provincial premier to be appointed rather than elected.

Alexander Cameron Rutherford had come to Alberta in 1895 after practising law for ten years in his native Ontario. He quickly became involved in the politics of the Northwest Territories. In 1902 he was elected as Strathcona's representative to the territorial assembly at Regina. Shortly afterward he was elected deputy speaker of the assembly.

In February, 1905 Prime Minister Laurier introduced a bill in the Canadian parliament to make Alberta a province. It passed, and G.H.V. Bulyea was named as Lieutenant-Governor.

By this time, Alex Rutherford was president of the Alberta Liberal Association. Lt.-Gov. Bulyea automatically appointed him the province's first premier. The method of selection was controversial, but a provincial election two months later confirmed Rutherford's position. The Liberals captured 23 seats out of 25.

One of the new government's first acts was to choose Edmonton as permanent capital of the province. This upset many of Rutherford's colleagues from southern Alberta who favoured Calgary as the capital. Calgarians, however, expected their city to be chosen as the site of the proposed provincial university.

But even this honour was denied Calgary. The cabinet decided to establish the university in Strathcona. Premier Rutherford personally selected the 293-acre site on the banks of the North Saskatchewan.

Education was a principal interest of Alex Rutherford. He attended the Imperial Conferences on Education in London in 1907 and 1911. He also considered the establishment of the University of Alberta his finest

17

achievement as premier.

There were other achievements, of course. He chose the site of the province's legislative building, for which he laid the cornerstone in 1909. His government established the provincial telephone system. He also helped found the Historical Society of Alberta.

Alberta's second provincial election was held in 1909. The Liberals won handily, 37 to 3. They had run under the slogan of "Rutherford, Reliability and Railways".

The "railways" part of that slogan came back to haunt the premier, however. A generous deal had been worked out between the provincial government and the American owners of the Alberta and Great Waterways Railways. The deal was criticized and a royal commission was appointed to investigate.

Premier Rutherford resigned in 1910 because of the railway scandal and because of bickering within his own cabinet. Some members were still sore about Edmonton being chosen both as the provincial capital and as the home of the university.

The royal commission cleared Premier Rutherford of any personal wrong-doing, but claimed he had failed to act in the best interests of the province. Rutherford was by now bitter about the opposition from within his own party, but ran again for the Liberals in 1913. He was defeated. In 1921 he campaigned for the Conservatives.

Among the honours A.C. Rutherford received during his life were doctorates from various Canadian universities, the King's Jubilee Medal and the title of honorary colonel of the 194th Highland Battalion. The greatest honour came in 1927, when he was appointed chancellor of the university he had founded. He held that position until his death in 1941 at the age of 84.

The Toronto *Globe* once described Alexander Cameron Rutherford as "an honest, upright figure in politics. A big man physically and mentally with a radiant humour in his eyes, and lines of stubborn strength finely blended in his genial face." A political foe who became a personal friend, Prime Minister R.B. Bennett, called him "an honest man, but over his head in politics."

A.C. Rutherford was a lover of books. After his death, most of his fine book collection was given to the University of Alberta. It is now housed in the Rutherford Library, named for the man known as the "father" of both the province and its university.

Frank Oliver

"Honest Frank," as his friends called him, was not only one of the first people to settle what is now Edmonton. He was largely responsible for putting it on the map.

He was born in Peel County, Ontario in 1853 and, while completing his high school education, worked on his father's farm and apprenticed as a printer with the local paper. He had some kind of disagreement with his father at that time, and changed his last name from Bowsfield to his mother's maiden name, Oliver. Frank spent the next few years continuing to work as a printer. In 1876, at the age of 23, he became captivated by the lure and promise of the West. Frank Oliver was obviously a man of vision and imagination, because there was nothing that seemed alluring or promising about Edmonton. It was then a collection of shacks and tents around a trading post a thousand miles from the nearest railroad. Frank pitched his tent where the University of Alberta now stands. Not intimidated by the mightiness of the Hudson's Bay Company, he opened a tiny rival trading store near the trading giant's Fort Edmonton. To get his supplies he made four hazardous trips to Winnipeg every year.

As Edmonton grew its people became interested in keeping in touch with world events.

Frank rose to the challenge and, on December 6, 1880, the first issue of the *Edmonton Bulletin*, a tiny 5-by-7-inch, 2-page weekly went to press.

Edmonton went through a series of booms and busts but it continued to grow, and Frank Oliver's paper grew along with it. "Read the Bible and the Bulletin" was its slogan and, in a number of ways, it served as a manifesto for the settlement and development of western Canada. Frank's editorials lashed out at the powers in Ottawa who "didn't give a damn" about the needs of westerners.

Frank Oliver, the fighter. In the early days of settlement, the federal government was slow in getting the land surveyed. Some homesteaders were fined or jailed for selling wood from their land

19

claims. They were also vulnerable to claim-jumpers moving onto their land. Frank was part of a group who took it upon themselves to push a claim-jumper's shack over the riverbank. He was arrested, but the jury found him not guilty.

Frank Oliver became the first representative elected to the North-west Territories Council, and played a major role in establishing Edmonton as the seat of government for Alberta. He was also responsible for getting the Territories their school law and election law. He was strongly opposed "to the Northwest being taxed by Ottawa, without being represented there, and to its local affairs and finances being conducted by Ottawa appointees instead of by the people of this country." For this reason, he chose to run for federal office, even though he probably could have become the first Premier of Alberta had he chosen. So, in 1876 he was elected to the federal house as an independent Liberal, and he later served in Prime Minister Laurier's cabinet. He became Minister of the Interior and Super-intendent of Indian Affairs.

He was not a handshaker or a baby-kisser, but throughout his 34-year political career he earned the love and respect of many. At the time of his death at age 80, he was still "in harness," and working as a member of the Board of Railway Commissioners. Perhaps the best testimony to Frank's faith and courage came from one of his close friends:

> "There was a man who would always fight for what he considered the right. They couldn't buy him, and they couldn't scare him."

The Grey Nuns

Mid-nineteenth-century western Canada, the fur traders would tell you, was "no place for white women, particularly those delicately reared in a convent." However, in 1859, Sister Lamy, Sister Alphonse and Sister Superior Leblanc Emery, stiff and bruised from their 85-day journey from Montreal, climbed out of their Red River cart at Lac Ste. Anne, Alberta. The first educated white women in western Canada, they belonged to the Institute of the Sisters of Charity, better known as the Grey Nuns.

They arrived in response to a plea from Bishop Provencher, who needed their help in ministering to the needs of the Native and Metis people. The fur trade had brought inter-tribal warfare, illicit

liquor traffic and diseases. A single smallpox epidemic, in 1869, spread through the Northwest like prairie fire wiping out one-half of Alberta's Indian population.

The sisters had their work cut out for them, and under extremely inhospitable living conditions.

Upon arriving at Lac Ste. Anne the sisters immediately learned Cree, and fifteen days later opened a school for 30 native students. Many of their students were in their early twenties, the same age as two of the sisters.

However, the threat of starvation soon made it impossible for them to continue their efforts in Lac Ste. Anne, so they moved to St. Albert, taking seven native orphan girls with them. The first convent was a log cabin loaned to them by Father Lacombe, O.M.I. They set up an orphanage as well as the Youville Residential School, which later expanded to include native students from five reserves.

The Grey Nuns' work in St. Albert also included establishing, in 1891, the first hospital in central Alberta, a frame structure attached to the mission. However, Edmonton was growing rapidly and diseases such as typhoid and smallpox, as well as pneumonia, blood poisoning and appendicitis, were taking their toll among the population.

In 1894, six young doctors asked the Grey Nuns to set up a General Hospital in Edmonton. The sisters moved fast. They purchased land from the Hudson's Bay Company, two of them lived in a shack on the grounds to oversee the construction and, in less than

21

a year, the hospital was ready to receive its first patients.

The activities of the Grey Nuns were not confined to the Edmonton area. They set up hospitals in Calgary, St. Paul, Cardston and Fort McMurray, and native schools in St. Paul, Cardston, Brocket and Fort Chipewyan. They established missions the full length of Canada, from Aklavik to Chesterfield Inlet; and in the United States, Japan, China, Haiti and Africa.

With new responsibilities the Grey Nuns moved with changing times. The directorship of their hospitals has passed on to the community. The Grey Nuns continue to serve their communities as social workers, teachers and nurses. The attitude that has guided their labours for centuries still prevails. "Ever on the threshold of want, yet never lacking in the essentials." It's an attitude that humanized the Canadian West.

Henry Marshall Tory

Premier Rutherford wanted a university. In 1908 he gave the job of creating it to a remarkable physics professor named Henry Marshall Tory. Classes began that September with 37 students. When Dr. Tory left 20 years later, the University of Alberta could boast six buildings and over 1,600 students.

Henry Marshall Tory was born on the Nova Scotia farm his great-grandfather had received for serving Britain during the American Revolutionary War. After a year of secondary education, he taught in the same kind of rural school which he himself had once attended.

Later, he went to McGill University in Montreal. The life of a scholar and educational pioneer had begun. In 1890 he won the university's gold medal in Mathematics and Physics.

He had also been active in student activities, especially debating. This Maritime farmboy, whose Scottish ancestors had supported Bonnie Prince Charlie, once *defended* the beheading of King Charles I. He presented his case so brilliantly that the subject was considered no longer debatable at McGill. Henry Tory was unanimously chosen top orator of his graduating class.

Next, he took a Bachelor of Divinity degree and spent two years preaching in a Montreal church. In 1893, however, he returned to McGill to lecture in Mathematics.

With an M.A. (1896) and a Doctorate in Science (1903), Dr. Tory became a roving ambassador of McGill. He set up a campus in Vancouver which later became part of the University of British Columbia. He also helped bring two Maritime colleges, Acadia and Mount Allison, into affiliation with McGill.

Then, for 20 years, his personality dominated the new University of Alberta. He frowned on student organizations which were not open to all, and so fraternities and sororities were not permitted. As a staunch Methodist, he was shocked when a new dance craze, the "one-step," hit the campus. A five-dollar fine was imposed on anyone caught performing it.

Under Dr. Tory, scientific research and adult education became trademarks of the university. He felt it was necessary to "take the university to the people." This same commitment to adult education took him to England to set up Canada's "Khaki College" for veterans of the First World War.

In 1928 Dr. Tory left Alberta to head Canada's National Research Council in Ottawa. It became one of the world's most important research organizations. In 1942 he took on the task of building another university, Carleton College in Ottawa. When he became president of Carleton, Dr. Tory was 79!

When Henry Marshall Tory died in 1947, Prime Minister King called him "an outstanding figure in fields of higher education and scientific research and of public service."

Perhaps the best assessment of his life came from Dr. Tory himself: "I am a pioneer!"

A.E. Cross

He was 23 years old and, like so many others of his day, he succumbed to the lure of the West. In 1884, Alfred Ernest Cross jumped on the C.P.R., and arrived in Calgary – one year after the railway. He worked as a bookkeeper, veterinarian and hired hand at a nearby ranch owned by Senator Cochrane. Having survived the trials of a hard winter and a wet and stormy spring, Cross then decided to strike out on his own.

By 1912 the Montreal-born graduate of eastern veterinary and agricultural schools had expanded his land holdings to become one of the largest individual ranch owners in Alberta. Part of his success was derived from his selection of the choicest varieties of cattle. In 1917, at a fair in Chicago, he received the highest price ever paid in the world market for grass-fed steers.

In 1888 a riding accident proved to be a turning point in his career. His doctor advised him to move to Calgary where medical assistance would be more readily available. This meant he had to turn his attention to a more urban-oriented enterprise.

Cross hit upon the ideal product – beer. For thirsty westerners who were tired of low-grade rotgut, it was a sure thing. So, Cross set about learning everything he could about breweries, studying and acquiring diplomas in Montreal, New York and Chicago. Thoroughly schooled in the art and science of beer production, he founded the Calgary Brewing and Malting Company. His first brew was so well-received by the men at the brewery and Mr. Cross's friends that, in "tasting" the batch, they ended up downing the whole lot.

As a prominent Calgary businessman, Cross had a hand in developing a number of companies. These included Canadian Western Natural Gas, Alberta Flour Mills, Royalite Oil and the Royal Trust Company. He was also one of the founding members of the Alberta Exhibition Association and a director of the Calgary General Hospital.

In his heart, however, he remained a rancher. Mr. Cross was active in what became the Western Stock Growers Association. This organization arose because the government appeared to be unconcerned with the problems of ranchers, who were experiencing conflicts over land leases and were suffering losses of their herds to wolves and cattle thieves.

In the election of 1899, he ran for the Conservative party in the East Calgary constituency and won. As a member of the Legislative Assembly for the Northwest Territories, he was active in the struggle to obtain provincial status for Alberta.

Alfred Ernest Cross, then, through his achievements as pioneer rancher, businessman and politician, was a key figure in the development of both the City of Calgary and the province as a whole.

Bob Edwards

As Bob Edwards once said, "It is well that there is no one without a fault for he would not have a friend in the world." For someone like Robert Chambers Edwards, a Scotsman who arrived in western Canada in 1894, the remark was revealing. He was both saint and sinner – widely admired for his brilliant honesty and despised by others for his lapses into "drunken degeneracy" and "libellous cynicism." Such extremes of character made him an ideal journalist in early Alberta.

The Wetaskiwin Free Lance was his first western Canadian paper, and was also the first newspaper between Calgary and Edmonton. He arrived in Alberta after working as a farmhand in Iowa, referring to Wetaskiwin as a place with "287 souls and three total abstainers." He wanted to call the paper

25

the "Wetaskiwin Bottling Works" but his friends advised against it. Opposition to his outrageous views caused him to move on, first to Leduc and then to Strathcona. There he started *The Alberta Sun*, once again bowing to convention by resisting naming it the "Strathcona Strathcolic." However, it was a difficult time for small-time newspaper editors and the struggle to keep the tiny paper going proved too much for him.

He therefore departed for Winnipeg and got a job as a staff writer for a Winnipeg daily. But working regular hours and meeting deadlines went against his freewheeling nature, so the rolling stone rolled to High River, Alberta. There, on March 4, 1902, the *Eye Opener* was born. However, his drinking habits and his editorial style brought him into conflict with the community's Methodist church. Discouraged, he came to Calgary and, in early 1904, his paper re-emerged as the *Calgary Eye Opener*.

There he finally found an audience who could appreciate the high quality of his writing, his humour and his criticism. He pulled no punches in his attacks on political figures, businessmen and socialites.

In many ways, however, he confused his readers. He was officially a Conservative, but was obviously a reformer. He lambasted the Church, but was a believer and practitioner of Christian charity. He was a self-confessed heavy drinker yet he supported prohibition. It is little wonder that people didn't know what to make of him.

His attacks on public figures, such as "the three biggest liars in Alberta are Robert Chambers, Gentleman; Hon. A.L. Sifton, Premier, and Bob Edwards, Editor," did not go down well with his hapless victims.

The fact that he always managed to avoid being sued for libel seemed miraculous. Ironically enough, he had occasion to launch a libel suit against the publisher of Calgary's *Daily News*, Mr. Daniel McGillicuddy. The latter, with whom he had had a running battle, had published a vindictive attack which hurt Edwards deeply. He enlisted the aid of his lawyer friend, Paddy Nolan, and a suit was launched. The verdict was technically in Edwards' favour but McGillicuddy got only a small fine and Edwards was reprimanded for publishing "debasing and demoralizing" material in his paper. It was such a disillusioning experience for Edwards that he decided to leave Calgary.

He remained in the East for two years but returned in 1911. The *Albertan* agreed to publish the *Eye Opener* and, once again, he was back in business, achieving the biggest circulation west of Toronto, excluding the Winnipeg dailies.

Two significant decisions in his life bore out his tendency to do the unexpected. First was in 1917 when, at the age of 53, he married, something he had sworn never to do. Bob declared, "When a man is in love for the first time, he thinks he invented it."

His second uncharacteristic action was to run for political office. He ran as an Independent candidate in the 1921 provincial election and won by a large majority, despite the fact that he made only one 60-second political speech. A statement he had once made turned out to be a prophecy. "Now I know what a statesman is; he is a dead politician, and what this country needs is more of them." Bob Edwards died in 1922, having served in the legislature for only one year. It is an irony that he would have appreciated.

William Fairfield

He was known as Alberta's agricultural trail blazer. Born in Titesville, Pennsylvania in 1867, William Harmon Fairfield was in the fifth generation of a family of British settlers who had come to the new world in 1630.

Agriculture had a strong appeal for William and he enrolled at the Colorado State Agriculture College and later at the University of Wyoming, receiving degrees in agriculture and horticulture.

Meanwhile, word of a boom in the Canadian West made its way south of the border and William and his brother Harry were intrigued by the prospect of testing their knowledge on the frontier farmland. "We just figured the cattle range and irrigation combination was for us," William later reported.

He established a ranch near Lethbridge which turned out to be a godsend for southern Alberta. He had the education and the expertise to follow through on many of the novel schemes put forth by William Pearce, a land surveyor referred to as 'the Father of Southern Alberta Irrigation'.

Charles Ora Card, Mormon leader in south-central and northern United States, approached Fairfield with his first challenge. Card's people had been trying unsuccessfully to grow alfalfa in the area. A return to Utah seemed imminent. William considered the problem and devised a procedure in which he "innoculated" the Alberta soil with soil from Wyoming upon which alfalfa had been grown successfully.

The Alberta Railway and Irrigation Company was so impressed with Fairfield's successful experiment that they purchased 400 acres for an experimental farm. They placed Fairfield in charge. Between 1905 and 1945, he devoted himself to the job. Through his efforts, farmers learned to farm effectively using irrigation, to break the land efficiently, to use suitable varieties of seeds and to plant and rotate their crops in a way that would produce the greatest yield. He discovered that adding sulphur to the grey-wooded soils of southern Alberta and Saskatchewan nearly doubled productivity.

Fairfield's work in the expansion of irrigation created a flourishing sugar beet industry in the province. Millions of trees now grace what was once bald prairie because he motivated local farmers to plant windbreaks on their land.

His vast contribution to agriculture earned him acclaim beyond his community, including an honorary doctor's degree from the University of Alberta in 1940. King George VI, in 1953, honoured him with membership in the Order of the British Empire for his service to agriculture and to humanity in general. Three years before his death, in 1961, hundreds of friends, colleagues, agricultural scientists, farmers, ranchers and businessmen gathered to commemorate his receiving of a fellowship in the Agricultural Institute of Canada, the association's highest honour. A fitting tribute to one who could claim to have done more for agriculture in southern Alberta than any other.

Tom Three Persons

When the Calgary Stampede made its debut in September, 1912, the public response was overwhelming. Despite continuous and heavy rains, twenty-four thousand spectators were there to enjoy the steer roping, the bulldogging, the trick ropers and the riders. There was a parade of trappers, prospectors, cowboys, Royal Northwest Mounted Police troops, buffalo teams, ox-teams and Indians, who completely surrounded the city with their tents and teepees.

Cowboys at that time did not wear the colourful hats, the satin

shirts, the flashy boots and the form-fitting jeans that we recognize today. It was the first big event for Calgary and the Canadian cowboys felt at a bit of a disadvantage competing with famous and experienced cowboys from all over the United States. However, there was one competitor that few local cowboys or the visitors had heard of.

His name was Tom Three Persons, a tall, handsome, 25-year-old Indian from Standoff on the Blood Reserve. A fine rider, he had been persuaded by his friends to enter the bronco-riding contest. But there was one small hitch. Moments before the contest was to begin, he was languishing in the Royal Northwest Mounted Police jail at Fort MacLeod for an unrecorded act of public mischief. As good fortune would have it, the Inspector of Indian Agencies made a plea to have Tom released in time to ride, and arranged to have a cash bond posted on his behalf. Tom was rushed to the Stampede Grounds just as the bronco-riding contest was getting underway.

The name of the horse he drew was Cyclone, a black, bucking, snorting and wild-eyed demon who had never been successfully ridden by anyone. Even his competitors were sympathetic. Cyclone's trick of rearing wildly, teetering on his hind legs and threatening to throw

29

himself backwards, had caused more than 125 of the world's best cowboys to hit the dirt. But Tom seemed unperturbed and his instincts told him that Cyclone was too clever to actually fall over, so he called the horse's bluff. Three Persons stayed on as Cyclone reared and spun and flipped from one end of the arena to the other. It was a ride to the finish, the first ever.

Bedlam broke out in the stands. A crowd surrounded Three Persons, congratulating him, for he was unquestionably the new holder of the World's Bronc Riding title. His native brothers made a great commotion; whooping and chanting and ecstatically circling the ring on their horses.

Meanwhile Tom had to return to jail, although his confinement was sweetened by the fact that he had won a medal, $1000 cash, a hand-made saddle and a champion belt with gold and silver mounted buckle.

This championship was to be Tom's chief claim to fame, although he was also an expert roper and continued to compete in rodeos in Calgary and elsewhere. He was a well-educated man, a promoter of progressive farming and ranching methods, and eventually became quite wealthy. At his ranch near Spring Coulee, he bred racing thoroughbreds, owned a large herd of Hereford cattle and supplied bucking broncos for rodeos at Lethbridge, Raymond, Cardston and Taber.

An unfortunate accident occurred in 1946 when Tom tried to prevent a young colt from breaking out of a corral. Three Persons broke his pelvic bone on a rail and was permanently disabled. From that point on his health declined and he eventually died at Calgary's Holy Cross Hospital in 1949 at age 63.

His funeral at St. Mary's Catholic Church was attended by cowboys, Indians, sportsmen and businessmen, the largest procession the Cardston church had ever witnessed. As reminders of his past glory, his photograph has a place of honour at the Blood reservation community hall at Standoff, and his beaded buckskins are on display at the Fort MacLeod museum.

Stephan G. Stephanson

He was born in 1853 on a small farm on the north coast of Iceland. The farm was on rocky ground but Stephan's early life was rich. Although his formal education stopped at elementary school, the Icelandic custom of nightly family reading acquainted him with his country's abundant literary heritage. It didn't take Stephan long to contribute to that heritage. He began writing poetry at age 15 and his first book of poems was published by age 19. By his early twenties, he was hailed as the leading Icelandic poet in North America.

He had no money when he arrived in Alberta and eked out a living by fishing, hunting and farming. Stephan also worked on a C.P.R. survey crew to make ends meet. It wasn't a particularly lucrative job as the surveyors were expected to pay for their room and board out of their $2.00 per day wages.

Despite his poverty, Stephan was an active man of the community. He was the first school board chairman of the Markerville School District and was one of the original organizers of the Tindastoll Butter and Cheese Manufacturing Company. The new venture became the first source of steady income for the Icelandic settlers.

Stephan considered himself a Canadian, although he retained his affection for his homeland. He continued writing poetry whenever he found a moment, and much of his poetry reflects his love for Canada. The following passage is from his poem "Toast to Alberta":

"Here veils of Northern Light are drawn
On high as winter closes,
And hoary dews at summer dawn
Adorn the wild red roses.
Sometimes the swelling clouds of rain
Repress the sun's caresses;
But soon the mountains smile again
And shake their icy tresses."

His scholarly life set him apart from the other people in his community and many of his opinions were unpopular among his contemporaries. He was deeply religious but was completely opposed to what he saw as the narrow-mindedness of the established churches.

In 1914 he became a bitter opponent of Canada's involvement in the First World War:

"In Europe's reeking slaughter-pen
They mince the flesh of murdered men,
While swinish merchants, snout in trough,
Drink all the bloody profits off!"

The other settlers in Markerville disapproved of Stephan for another reason as well. In their view, he was too fond of socializing and burdened his wife Helga with the responsibility of raising their five sons and three daughters.

Stephan's fellow settlers may have misunderstood him but they bought his books and were proud of his fame.

Following his death they dedicated a community park to his memory and established the Stephan G. Stephanson Chapter of the Icelandic Society. His farmhouse still stands, a shrine for Icelandic people everywhere. It has since become an Alberta Government historical site.

Throughout his life Stephanson's fondest hope was to move people through his poetry:

"And when the last of all my days is over,
The last page turned,
And whatsoever shall be deemed in wages
That I have earned;
In such a mood I hope to be composing
My sweetest lay;
And then – extend my hand to all the world
And pass away."

Archibald Wayne Dingman

It started with the discovery of a well at Turner Valley and became the "Fantastic Calgary Oil Boom" of 1914. It was a spark which ignited nearly 400 new companies, emerging overnight in the expectation of big profits from oil. One oil historian later reported that "on Friday, every available motor vehicle in Calgary was forced into service, carrying hundreds of men to the foothills and the Dingman well."

The discovery well produced many other notable changes as well. Steel derricks replaced wooden ones. Twelve thousand producing wells and a bewildering array of special machines for production and distribution completely altered Alberta's pastoral landscape.

This extraordinary turn of events was set in motion by a man who once sold soap for a living.

But he was born with a talent for business, and as a child growing up in Greenbush, Ontario in the late 1850s and 60s, Dingman educated himself on a variety of subjects which were to prove useful later on. He was one of nine children from a United Empire Loyalist family and, as soon as he came of age, he headed for the developing Pennsylvania oil fields in the 1880s. It was there that he gained his first business experience in the oil industry. When he later returned to his homeland, his thoughts of searching for oil in Canada were discouraged for a variety of reasons, mainly financial. In the meantime, he became involved in a company that manufactured coaster brakes for bicycles. He also worked for the Scarborough Electric Railway,  and his strong interest in electric lighting led him to become associated with the first company to install electric lights in Toronto and other cities. In fact, he was later to claim that he personally placed the first electric streetlight in Toronto.

His involvement with the soap company which would have made him a millionaire was cut short when the company burned to the ground in the great Toronto fire in 1900.

This calamity, along with his never-extinguished interest in searching for oil, led him to Calgary in 1902. In his quest for oil there were numerous obstacles to overcome: pioneering difficulties. The roads leading to what might prove to be an oil-bearing well were pot-holed and almost impassable. There was a pathetic shortage of field equipment, and what there was had to be imported from the United States. There were frequently long delays in its arrival. The availability of geological data, let alone experienced wildcatters, was also severely limited. Further, the fact that markets for gas and oil were almost completely undeveloped meant that the all-important dollar was a constant source of worry.

But Dingman was one of those who persevered and, in 1905,

organized the Calgary Gas Company. His first well on the Sarcee Indian Reserve, although he optimistically declared a holiday thinking he had finally made it, proved unsuccessful.

The Walker Well, his company's second attempt, did contain gas in sufficient quantities to provide domestic fuel and street lighting in East Calgary, after initially providing gas to the Calgary Brewing and Malting Company.

This success led him to pursue oil exploration in a big way and he formed the Calgary Petroleum Products Company in 1912. It was this company that drilled the history-making well in Turner Valley.

Dingman was a tireless worker and was hard at it until about two weeks prior to his death at 85. Even then, he had mapped out twenty years of future work in oil exploration. He also proved to be a prophet as well as an oilman. His lifelong slogan was "Carry on, we want and need more crude oil."

James Bertram Collip

The discovery of insulin is popularly associated with the names Banting and Best. There were two other Canadians connected with the medical breakthrough in diabetes. One was Professor Macleod of the University of Toronto, and the other was an Albertan – James Bertram Collip.

Dr. Collip's contribution was to make insulin available for therapeutic use. He developed a technique using alcohol to remove toxic substances from it and to preserve it. Although he won the Nobel Prize for this work with Banting, Best and Macleod, he felt his share of the discovery "was only that which any well-trained biochemist would be expected to contribute." This modesty was characteristic.

He was above all a scientist, and a dedicated one. His early education was in a one-room country school in Belleville, Ontario, where he qualified to attend Trinity College at the University of Toronto by age 15. By the time he was 23, he had his PhD in Biochemistry. In 1915, the University of Alberta offered him his first academic appointment as a lecturer in Physiology and Biochemistry. He was a shy man and wasn't particularly comfortable standing in front of students. He also managed to pursue his personal research, often working through the night. His wife Ray, whom he had met at Trinity College, would often join him in the evenings to keep him company.

In 1921 Dr. Collip received a Rockefeller Travelling Fellowship to go to Toronto to work on carbohydrate metabolism with Dr. Macleod. It was there that the fateful connection with Drs. Banting and Best occurred.

He became fascinated with the new field of endocrinology, the study of glands that secrete hormones throughout the bloodstream.

He got an opportunity to return to the University of Alberta as Professor of Biochemistry in 1922, and decided to enter the Faculty of Medicine at the same time. He felt it would better equip him to understand the ways in which hormones affect the human body. He discovered a method of extracting a hormone from the parathyroid glands and his finding provided relief for patients suffering from spasms of the voluntary muscles (parathyroid tetany). His methods soon became standard procedure in clinical laboratories throughout the world.

Although Collip had special fondness for Alberta (his three children were born in Edmonton), his particular brand of genius and integrity was in great demand. Therefore, in 1928 he was invited to go to McGill University to assume the Chair of Biochemistry. There he discovered that certain chemicals in the bloodstream affect people's personalities as well as their growth, their complexion and their energy level.

Collip was also responsible for inventing a method of blood preservation, which was of great benefit in providing emergency relief for the wounded.

He received the Flavelle gold medal for distinguished work in the field of natural science as well as honorary degrees from virtually every university in Canada and a number in England and the United States. However, the friend who gave the eulogy at James Collip's funeral pointed out that a full life requires more than honorary bouquets: "We remember the intuitions which guided his experiments, the speed and fairness of his decisions and the velocity of his movements, his swiftness to praise and reluctance to blame, his timidity in his own defence and his fury in protection of his friends."

Emily Murphy

She was a pretty girl, bubbly and bright-eyed, had the nickname "Sunshine" and the brains to go with it.

Emily Ferguson graduated from the Bishop Strachan School in Toronto with a medal for general proficiency. While she was at school, she met a theology student named Arthur Murphy, whom she married at age 19. Arthur's outstanding ability as a preacher soon led to a position in London with a British missionary society. Emily found herself having to defend Canadians to the rather disdainful British and earned herself the nickname "Janey Canuck." Later she adopted this as her pen-name when the couple returned to Canada.

Her writing career started to flourish. They moved to Swan Lake, Manitoba in 1904 and it was there she wrote book reviews for the *Winnipeg Telegram* and her collection of articles on pioneer life called *Janey Canuck in the West* became a best-seller. At the same time, she was responsible for managing their 320-acre farm, while Arthur was occupied in the timber business.

When the Murphys moved to Edmonton in 1907, her interests became increasingly political. It seemed that she succeeded at whatever she took on. One important victory was the passage of *The*

Dower Act, a piece of legislation which gave women a share in their husbands' homesteads. Her demands for a court that dealt exclusively with women's problems were also successful. Emily Murphy was appointed Magistrate.

She seemed stern and forbidding in her office but her fundamental viewpoint was that lawbreakers should be rehabilitated rather than punished.

One lawyer, Eardly Jackson, refused to accept her judgments, because she was not legally a "person." Other lawyers followed suit, but the Alberta Supreme Court upheld her authority. Still, at the federal level, women could not be admitted to the Senate because the British North America Act did not recognize them as "persons."

Emily found herself embroiled in a battle which "took me thirteen years and almost broke my heart." Despite a vigorous press campaign, and the support of Canadian women's groups, the federal government did nothing to change the situation. Eventually she initiated an appeal to the Supreme Court of Canada, along with four other women – Nellie McClung, Irene Parlby, Henrietta Edwards and Louise McKinney. This also failed. The last resort was the Privy Council of England. Finally, in 1929, it was decreed that women were indeed persons.

Ironically, the success of this judgment contained within it the greatest disappointment of Emily's career. Emily was an obvious choice for senator, but was overlooked for a variety of reasons. One senator explained, "Oh, we never could have had Mrs. Murphy in the Senate! She would have caused too much trouble."

She did indeed cause trouble – exposing the evils of the narcotics trade in a world-renowned book called *The Black Candle*. She also promoted birth control at a time when such a thing was unheard-of.

Immediately before her death, she visited the court where she had served for seventeen years. On that occasion someone said of her, "We are honoured today by the presence of Mrs. Emily Murphy, Police Magistrate and Judge. A feminine note missing from this building...is brought back by the kindly, smiling countenance of this beloved lady." The speaker was none other than Eardly Jackson, the lawyer who had repeatedly challenged her authority years before.

William Pearce

The career of William Pearce, "Czar of the Prairies," spanned an era of high adventure, dramatic change and big ideas.

Born in Elgin County, Ontario, in 1848, he started his government duties as a land surveyor. For Pearce, this meant travelling to unsettled areas of the west by dog team and sleeping under sled dogs for

warmth. It also meant living on wild meat, hard tack, pemmican and tea. He was a big man, well-suited to this rugged life. Once when he fell into a frozen river, narrowly escaping drowning, he discovered that the layer of ice on top of his clothing provided good insulation against the cold. He tried to persuade the other men in his party to do the same. They were not interested.

In over 30 years as a land surveyor throughout the then Northwest Territories, Pearce became very familiar with both the issues and the resources of western Canada, prior to the creation of the new province.

Pearce was responsible for attracting the attention of the Dominion government to the need for irrigation in the future southern Alberta. At first the government was not receptive to his ideas. Potential settlers might be discouraged if the government itself admitted that water was in short supply. Nonetheless, Pearce persevered.

Once, when he was making a presentation to the government, some of the Members of Parliament claimed to be ignorant of exactly what irrigation was. The exasperated Mr. Pearce suggested that taking a look at the lawn sprinklers on the Parliament grounds might help clarify things for them.

Back home he made a public example of the benefits of irrigation by piping water from Bragg Creek onto his land in East Calgary. His neighbours were astounded by the quality and quantity of grains and vegetables this produced.

Severe drought in southern Alberta in the 1890s strengthened Pearce's case, and his efforts were eventually rewarded with the passage of *The Northwest Irrigation Act* in 1894. A number of the irrigation projects promoted by Pearce were ahead of their time. One of these was the present-day Bassano Dam, which he proposed because the C.P.R. was having problems getting enough water for running its locomotives in the southern part of the province. As Pearce phrased it, "We could get water from the eastern area, for locomotives, for irrigation, and for stock watering purposes. We could change the face of the country."

An ambitious idea, which came to be known as the "William Pearce Scheme," foreshadowed the Alberta government's PRIME plan. Pearce claimed that by taking water from the North Saskatchewan, Clearwater and Red Deer rivers and storing it in Sullivan Lake, it could be possible to irrigate over a million acres in central Alberta and west-central Saskatchewan. He was convinced the idea was completely practical. It terrified government officials of his time, and it is still controversial today.

Pearce was also outspoken about the conservation of natural resources – an idea which few of his contemporaries understood. William Van Horne, president of the C.P.R. and personal friend of Pearce, was an exception. When Pearce was a member of the Dominion Lands Board, Van Horne encouraged him to reserve ten square miles around the Banff Hot Springs as government land. This small beginning opened the door to Canada's system of national parks.

William Pearce was a man of great schemes and grandiose imaginings. His sandstone mansion in East Calgary had fifteen rooms and three fireplaces. It was affectionately referred to by Calgarians as the "Bow Bend Shack." Pearce would have been disappointed to know that it was torn down in 1957. He had intended it as a monument, built to last forever.

Alberta's parks and irrigation programs and resource development reflect much more effectively his concern for the needs of future generations.

William Griesbach

William Antrobus Griesbach was born to be a soldier. His father, equally military, was the first man to join the Royal Northwest Mounted Police.

The future Canadian General was born at Fort Qu'Appelle, Saskatchewan in 1878. In 1899 he served with the Canadian Mounted Rifles in the South African War. He was a slight man, weighing only 138 pounds, but he used his ingenuity to attain the 140-pound military requirement by concealing a two-pound lump of coal behind his back while being weighed. He also astounded the military doctors with what they thought was his extraordinary eyesight. William had committed to memory the calendar which they used in the examination, including the fine print. Enroute overseas, he passed through Regina and there approached the Benchers of the Law Society of the Territories to permit him a pass for his final examination in law. Although he had not read all of the prescribed books, he managed to confound the Benchers with a discussion on wills that lasted the entire examination period. He was thereby admitted to the Bar at age 22 and later became the senior member of the law firm of Griesbach and O'Connor.

When he returned from South Africa, he became an alderman in Edmonton in 1905. Two years later, at the age of 29, he was elected mayor. Griesbach felt that city council members should be paid businessmen's salaries. This opinion was not particularly popular with voters, but bowing to the views of others was not a concern of Griesbach's.

On two occasions, in 1905 and 1913, he attempted to get elected as a Conservative member of the provincial legislature, and was defeated both times. His attempt to get elected to the federal House of Commons in 1911 was equally unsuccessful.

However, on the outbreak of the Great War in 1914 he volunteered for service in the Canadian Expeditionary Force and quickly distinguished himself. He led the 49th Battalion in active duty in France.

Soldiers of the Battalion remember him as hard, but very just; never forcing them into battlefield conditions he was unwilling to risk himself. For his outstanding military service he was decorated with the Distinguished Service Order (D.S.O.) and bar.

After returning from overseas, he again ran for federal office in the 1917 election, against Liberal incumbent, Frank Oliver. His opponent bitterly commented on Griesbach's candidacy in *The Bulletin:*

"That Col. Griesbach returned from England to Canada in the supposed interests of the Conservative Party rather than in the interests of the Empire is made amply evident by the acceptance of the party nomination for West Edmonton...Clearly...he was thought to be a party necessity if there was to be a hope of carrying the constituency for the government."

It did nothing to halt Griesbach's political career. In 1921, at the age of 44, he was appointed to the Senate by Prime Minister Arthur Meighen. Twenty years later he became Inspector-General of Western Canadian Forces.

In the years prior to his death in 1945, he wrote his autobiography entitled *I Remember*. The book shows an entirely different side to "Billy" Griesbach. He reveals himself as a rare and witty man, with the ability to laugh at his own mistakes.

1919 - 1929

A Fresh Furrow

Young farm boys returned from the Great War in Europe (1914 - 1918) impatient with the old order and bewildered by change that had already come to Alberta. Inflation, unemployment, prohibition and bitter political wars greeted the returning soldiers. The grim tensions eased with prosperity and significant political change.

Henry Wise Wood

He was acclaimed "The Uncrowned King of Alberta" and "The Moses of Alberta Farmers." Henry's father served in the Confederate army and was a prosperous farmer in Missouri, where Henry was born in 1860. In the fashion of that place and time, his father was also a slave-owner, although Henry remembered the slaves as being treated more like members of the family.

Henry Wise Wood's earliest ambition was to enter the ministry. But in the 1890s he became involved in the Farmers' Equity Movement, an organization dedicated to promoting the rights of farmers. His own farming operations in both Missouri and Texas were very successful. However, at the age of 45, he saw Alberta as an opportunity to fulfill his boyhood dream of becoming a cowboy. Alberta had just become a province and, to him, it was the "finest in the world."

Henry Wise Wood maintained there was "no use holding a membership of citizenship unless one is going to use it." In 1909 he joined the United Farmers of Alberta (U.F.A.), and in 1911 he took out his Canadian citizenship. In both cases, his commitment was whole-hearted.

At the time Alberta farmers had had to accept what the buyer was willing to pay for their products. Henry's answer was "Organize! You will never get anything in this world that you do not get for yourself." Through Henry's efforts, Alberta farmers gained a sense of their own value. As a result, some 30,000 Alberta farmers became united; a force to be reckoned with, both provincially and federally.

Wise Wood was also a pivotal figure in the creation of wheat pools in Alberta. "If the government will not provide a wheat board, the farmers...can create their own." Wheat pools gave farmers control over the marketing of their grain and thanks to Wise Wood the Alberta Wheat Pool was formed in 1923. He also helped farmers in Saskatchewan and Manitoba establish their own wheat pools. Wise Wood had a vision of farmers from Argentina, Australia and the United States uniting with Canadian farmers in a common purpose.

Wise Wood was opposed to the U.F.A. becoming a political party, feeling it would undermine the organization's grass roots strength. Other members disagreed and urged that the U.F.A. run candidates in the 1921 election. Henry bowed to the will of the majority and dropped everything in order to work on the campaign. The U.F.A. formed the government and Wise Wood seemed the logical choice for premier. But he declined political office, although many considered him the most influential man in Alberta throughout the 1920s.

Fred Brewster

He lived for nearly 70 years in the Rockies. The title "Gentleman of the Mountains" was well deserved. The mountains were his lifeblood, his greatest passion. Frederick Archibald Brewster came by his attachment honestly. His father John once said, "Most people are hemmed in by clocks and timetables and their molehills become mountains. The first time they see a mountain they put the molehill in its proper place." In 1887, when Fred was three years old, the Brewsters moved to Banff. The family was to figure prominently in such tourist enterprises as Banff's Mount Royal Hotel, the

Kananaskis Dude Ranch and the Brewster Transport Company.

Fred had to leave the mountains briefly to complete his high school education at St. John's College in Winnipeg and to obtain a mining engineer's degree at Queen's University in Kingston. But he couldn't leave them behind forever and made his home in Jasper. When he was twenty years old, he and a companion spent a full year packing and canoeing through the Cariboo country.

He wintered at Finlay River under conditions to discourage the average mortal. In Fred's mind, "the stars always shone brightly and seemed very near in the mountain air. Otherwise we were alone in a mighty world of peaks, glaciers and snow."

His knowledge of the mountains was sought out by such organizations as the Smithsonian Institute and the United States Department of Biological Survey. He led explorers and hunting parties, tracking down ranges of big game and researching and collecting specimens north of the Yellowhead Pass. On one of these trips Brewster and his party established the northern boundary of the Rocky Mountain Big Sheep Range. On another journey, he discovered the dominant mountain west of Grande Prairie. He named it Mount Sir Alexander, after the first white man to travel through the Rockies.

It was a personal crusade of Brewster that tribute should be paid to fur trade explorers like Thompson, Fraser and others who risked their lives exploring new lands. They made history. In turn, he noted that Jasper House, Howse Pass, Jasper Lake, Jasper Park Lodge and Jasper National Park were named after an obscure fur trade book-keeper named Jasper Howse. Brewster was irked that the Indian name for Jasper National Park, "The Land of Glittering Mountains" was replaced by a white man's name.

Fred returned from a trip to discover that the First World War was underway. He immediately joined the Second Tunneling Division of the Canadian Engineers. Swiftly he rose to the rank of Major and in 1917 was decorated with the Military Cross and Bar.

After the war he returned to Jasper and set about making the mountains more accessible to visitors. He helped blaze new trails for horseback trips, including the Skyline Trail to Maligne Lake. Fred Brewster was a familiar to thousands of visitors from across Canada, the United States and Europe; people whom he guided on big game hunts, trail rides and long hikes through back country by ski and snow-shoe.

He remained a cross-country skier and vigorous walker until very late in life and lived to the age of 85. Appropriately, he was buried in the cemetery in Jasper, surrounded by his beloved mountains.

"There seems no end to this vast, white land. But it

is not a dead land. It is very much alive – alive with veins of fire that glint in the sun."

Irene Parlby

When Mary Irene Marryat first came to Alberta she was fresh from a background that included a continental education and a life of ease among the aristocracy of England and British India. Even though she had to learn such tasks as cooking, cleaning, washing and ironing from scratch, she was captivated by the quiet open spaces and the fellowship among the scattered souls in her community. Besides, she saw life in Alix as an opportunity to make her own way. She had met and married Walter Parlby, a graduate of Oxford who shared her love of gardening, literature and theatre. The new English bride caused some talk in Alix with her fondness for pretty clothes, bronco riding, fine china and buckskins.

However, she was well aware that the lives of her neighbours were much less stimulating than her own. She became involved in setting up a women's group for mutual help and education. The group evolved into the Women's Auxiliary of the United Farmers of Alberta. The community women's circle became a province-wide organization.

Irene felt "farm women realize there are other things of interest in the world, and that they do their housekeeping all the better for thinking of outside affairs."

These turned out to be prophetic words that hurled Irene into the political arena. The United Farmers of Alberta were transforming from an economic pressure group into a political party. Irene was asked to run for office in the Lacombe riding in the 1921 election. She won, and the U.F.A. formed the government.

The experience was an eye-opener. "I never realized until my first campaign in 1921 what miserable, incompetent creatures women were in the eyes of the public. I ought to have developed a terrible inferiority complex by the time it was over, for practically the only issue that seemed to concern the electorate or the opposition, was that I was a woman and worse, an English woman.

Irene was concerned with other issues. Her persuasiveness, humanitarian ideals and good judgment earned her the respect of her male colleagues. She was selected Minister Without Portfolio in Premier Herbert Greenfield's cabinet, the second woman in the British Empire to be so appointed.

While her portfolio was officially unnamed, her responsibilities were very clear in her own mind. She fought to improve laws affecting the lives of women and children. These included legislation to provide municipal hospitals, public health nurses, child welfare clinics, minimum wages for women, property rights for married women and immigration laws to prevent settlers from being exploited. She was also a member of the 'Famous Five' who gave Canadian women the right to be officially considered 'persons' and eligible as members of the Canadian Senate.

Her greatest interest was "education, education and more education" and she was involved in projects to upgrade the schooling of all children. Her dedication led to an honorary Doctor of Laws degree from the University of Alberta, another first for Canadian women.

Despite her successes, Irene Parlby found much of the talk and paperwork associated with political office boring and disillusioning. She once confessed that, having left public life, she was strongly tempted to throw all the political documents and papers into a huge bonfire and dance around it.

However, after the exhausting 1930 election campaign (another aspect of public life she considered a waste of time), she was asked by Prime Minister Bennett to represent Canada at a League of Nations meeting in Geneva. Her Alberta supporters persuaded her to continue in office until the end of her term in 1935.

In private life, her services as a public speaker and writer continued to be in great demand and she pursued these interests until her death in 1969 at the age of 97.

Her leadership in fighting for women's rights, education and improvement of welfare benefits links her with a proud tradition of Alberta women pioneers.

Nellie McClung

Some called her "Windy Nellie," "Calamity Nell," "Holy Terror" and "The Hyena in Petticoats." The Manitoba Conservatives once burned her in effigy.

The real Nellie Letitia Mooney McClung was an attractive, warm-hearted, humorous woman. She was born the youngest of six children of an Irish immigrant farm family in Ontario in 1873.  The Mooneys moved to Wawanesa, Manitoba when Nellie was six years old. At that time the tiny community had no school, which meant that she didn't learn to read until she was ten years old. However, her ability as a student proved outstanding and she became a qualified teacher and novice writer by the time she was sixteen.

From a very early age she challenged the inequality between the sexes and found an ally in Wes McClung, the son of a minister. Her mother-in-law, Mrs. McClung, encouraged Nellie to pursue her writing, and this led to publication of her first novel, *Sowing Seeds in Danny*.

Her mentor encouraged Nellie to read sections of the book at meetings of the Women's Christian Temperance Union (W.C.T.U.), which gave the young bride her first invaluable experience in public speaking.

Nellie became involved in the Winnipeg Political Equality League, an organization dedicated to securing the vote for women. When conventional methods failed, drastic measures were in order. The result was a Women's Mock Parliament, staged at Winnipeg's Walker Theatre. In the play, men were put in the position of being denied the vote. Nellie's speech brought down the house in gales of laughter:

"The trouble is that if men start to vote, they will vote too much. Politics unsettles men, and unsettled men means unsettled bills, broken furniture, broken vows and divorce...If men were to get into the habit of voting, who knows what might happen – it's hard enough to keep them at home now."

The play was successful and so was the argument. In 1916 Manitoba women received the vote.

Nellie's activities in the suffrage movement carried her throughout North America. Neighbours hinted darkly that she neglected her children and that her marriage was hovering near divorce. It was far from true. Her marriage was a happy one and her husband applauded her activities. As a joke, he trained their son to respond to anti-suffragists with the line, "My name is Mark McClung. My mother is a suffragist and I have never known a mother's love."

In 1921, shortly after the family moved to Alberta, Nellie was elected to the legislature as a Liberal member of the Opposition. Irene Parlby sat on the opposite side of the house as a member of the United Farmers of Alberta party.

Together they supported social welfare causes such as public health nurses, municipal hospitals, liberalized property laws for women and improved health and education for school children. Both joined with Emily Murphy in the famous "Persons Case" to give women the official right as "persons" to become members of the Canadian Senate.

She never backed down from anything she believed in – "Never retract, never explain, never apologize; get the thing done and let them howl!" She handled her political defeat in 1926 by embarking on a "baking binge" and then got on with her family life and her writing.

Nellie McClung was the first Canadian, male or female, to make a living as an author. Prior to her death in Victoria in 1951 at age 68, she had published sixteen books, as well as innumerable magazine and newspaper articles.

Her eloquent arguments in favour of women's liberation, in fact human liberation, could easily have been written today:

"The time will come, we hope, when women will be economically free, and mentally and spiritually independent enough to refuse to have their food paid for by men, when women will receive equal pay for equal work, and have all avenues of activity open to them; and will be free to choose their own mates, without shame, or indelicacy; when men will not be afraid of marriage because of the financial burden, but free men and free women will marry for love, and together work for the sustenance of their families."

Karl Clark

Peter Pond, the first white trader to travel down the Athabasca River, was impressed by tar sands and remarked on them in his diaries. "They have been a taunt to North America for generations. They wear a smirk which seems to say: When are you going to do something?" Karl Adolph Clark was speaking of the Athabasca tar sands and spent his lifetime answering their challenge. Clark got his first opportunity to "do something" in 1920, when Dr. Henry Marshall Tory invited him to join the newly-formed Research Council of Alberta. He was asked to head up the Road Materials Section, which involved working out a method to utilize the oil sands for paving roads. It was a pioneering effort for which Clark was well-qualified. He had been working as Chief Road Materials Engineer for the Canadian government.

When he arrived in Edmonton, he began research which was to effect tar sands extraction not only in Alberta, but all over the world. The technique he evolved is known as the "water flotation extraction method." In simple language it involved mixing strip-mined, oil bearing sand with hot water and then skimming off the bitumen tar when it rose to the surface. The tar was put through further extraction and refining processes, to obtain a usable product called "synthetic crude."

But he continued with his investigation of the tar sands on his own. When World War II arrived and large amounts of oil were needed to meet war-time needs, the Research Council was quickly resurrected. Dr. Clark began researching other aspects of petroleum extraction. The government financed the construction of an extraction plant at Bitmount on the Athabasca River. Dr. Clark's hot-water process proved very successful. Major oil companies became interested in the Athabasca oil sands.

Great Canadian Oil Sands (G.C.O.S.) decided to act, and Dr. Clark became central to their operation. He soon became an international advisor to industry and government.

Despite his achievements, Dr. Clark remained a modest man who gave equal credit to those who had helped him with his work. He retained his office at the Research Council (taking his cocker spaniel with him to work every day) and continued finding solutions to oil sands problems.

For a man who had committed three decades of his life to oil research, the greatest reward would have been to see the G.C.O.S. plant go into operation. It occurred in 1967, a year after his death.

J. Percy Page

Most people, when they think about the years they spent in school, can remember at least one teacher who set what seemed impossibly high standards.

J. Percy Page, who taught commercial education in the Edmonton school system for forty years, was that kind of teacher. And he got results.

He also demanded impeccable behaviour from his pupils, as one girl who was caught sliding down the school bannister discovered. "Young ladies in my school do not slide down bannisters!"

However, young ladies at his school did play basketball. In 1914 a group of girls asked him if he would coach their team. He said he would give it a try and began drilling his players in shooting and passing during two weekly 90-minute practice sessions. By the end of their first year, the Commercial Grads walked off with the City Championship.

From then on, there was no looking back. Page inspired clean, simple plays, and the "Grads," over a period of twenty-five years, won 502 out of 522 games. They travelled the globe, played at four Olympic meets, and held the world title for seventeen consecutive years.

But once World War II began, the fifth Olympic meet was

cancelled. Also, the Grads' arena, the Edmonton Gardens, was taken over by the Air Commonwealth training force. 1940 was the final year for the Grads – the team with the greatest record in sports history. As for Percy Page, he went on to become principal of the commercial section at Victoria Composite High School. When he retired in 1952, he was quoted as "wondering what I'll do with my time." The answer came four days later when he became house leader for the Alberta Progressive Conservative party. It wasn't his first foray into politics. He had long been active in citizens' associations and had sat in the legislature as an independent member. Throughout his political life he lobbied for reforms which favoured "the little guy": reducing federal taxes, making the provincial government responsible for health and social assistance programs. He felt the Social Credit party policy of subsidizing oil companies was not benefitting the people of Alberta. He also accused the Manning government of "railroading" pupils through Alberta high schools, claiming the system was "not producing the educated men and women the province needed."

Page was defeated in the 1959 provincial election, but shortly thereafter Prime Minister John Diefenbaker appointed him Lieutenant-Governor of Alberta. In 1954 Prime Minister Lester Pearson extended his term. He continued in that office until his retirement in 1966.

At the time of Page's death at age 85, a close friend described him as a man "standing on tiptoe...the better to discover what life is really all about."

Roland Gissing

The beauty of Alberta's scenery – its mountains, its foothills and its prairies – is now world-famous. Much of the credit for this acclaim must go to an artist named Roland Gissing, whose paintings hang in galleries throughout North America and Europe. Reproductions of his work also adorn calendars, Christmas cards and book illustrations around the world.

Gissing came to Alberta from his native England in 1913, when he was just sixteen years old. He had seen American movies of the wild west, and his greatest dream was to be a cowboy. At first, he had to settle for a job looking after ponies for a polo club near Calgary. But he bought a pair of cowboy chaps with his first pay cheque, and managed to get hired on as a cowhand at a ranch near Crossfield. He continued riding the range for the next ten years, sketching ranch scenes along the way. It wasn't until he settled near Cochrane in the mid-1920s that he began taking his painting seriously. He educated himself by studying great masters. In 1929 this work culminated in a very successful one-man show at an art gallery in Calgary. However,  with the arrival of the Great Depression, Gissing's plans to open his own studio met with financial disaster. He was forced to get work decorating the walls of the Hudson's Bay Cafeteria and the Club Cafe.

He soon returned to Cochrane, got married and resumed his painting. He would spend his summer days sketching, going into the mountains and remaining for weeks at a time. During the winter he would paint, usually in oils.

Gissing also developed a passion for model railroads, which he made entirely by hand. The engines actually worked, and one locomotive could pull more than a ton!

In 1944 his home and studio, which he had largely built himself, were completely destroyed by fire. He felt the loss of his model railroad even more keenly than the destruction of his books and paintings. However, he picked up the pieces, rebuilt a new home and studio, and carried on.

Gissing, unlike most artists, was recognized by the international art community during his lifetime. By the time he reached middle age, art connoisseurs were eager to obtain "early Gissings" for their private collections. One "early Gissing," an enormous 6' by 8' painting of a buffalo hunt, once decorated the outside wall of a service station in Banff!

The artist himself was a quiet, modest man who used his painting to help him come to terms with his greatest love, nature. Although the Rocky Mountains personally intimidated him, he always portrayed them as restful.

His landscapes speak a language that everyone can understand and enjoy, and his work has brought delight to thousands of people throughout the world.

Herman Trelle

The Peace River district wasn't always considered a fertile agricultural belt. But Herman Trelle once boasted it could grow everything except grapefruit. And he almost proved it.

Along the way, he also picked up some 135 championships for various crops including wheat, oats and field peas. He put the Peace River Country onto the world agricultural map.

He was educated in Edmonton and on family trips to Germany. His first championship wasn't in agriculture, but in public speaking when, at 17, he became Edmonton's top boy orator.

Engineering studies at the University of Alberta were cut short by the First World War. To his bitter disappointment, his German-American background disqualified him from wartime service, so he followed his parents to Peace River and began farming.

In 1918 he made another attempt to enlist, this one successful. No sooner had he joined the Royal Flying Corps, however, than the war ended.

Back on the farm he began experimenting with cross-breeding strains of wheat. He soon concentrated on varieties of the Marquis wheat which had proven so successful on the Canadian prairies. By 1920 he was growing his own registered grain, and six years later he captured the world wheat championship in Chicago. The same year his Victory oats took the world honours. Herman Trelle continued his experiments, branching out into hybrid projects involving flowers, vegetables and fruit. In 1928 the Alberta government set aside a farm near Wembley for his various testing programs. Poor health plagued Herman Trelle periodically, but this did not prevent him from showing off his farm to visitors. His health did keep him away from the world wheat championships in 1929, but he made up for it by winning the award in each of the next three years.

In 1932 he was barred from contesting the world wheat title for three years because he had won it too often. As soon as he became eligible again, in 1936, he was once more named top world wheat grower.

Although Trelle complained that he didn't make much money as a championship grower, he certainly earned an international reputation. He was not modest about any of his achievements, either. He once bragged to the dean of the U. of A. agricultural school that he could talk in ten languages. "You know, Herman," the dean replied, "you should learn to keep quiet in ten languages."

In World War II he enlisted with the Royal Canadian Engineers and served briefly in Ontario before being discharged for medical reasons. The overseas duty he wanted eluded him for good.

Herman Trelle never returned to farming. After two years as a munitions inspector with the C.P.R. in Calgary, he moved to California. A few months later, as supervisor of ranch holdings for the Overholtz Company, the world-famed grower met a tragic death.

He was shot and fatally wounded by a ranch-hand whom he had fired the day before.

Jimmy Simpson

Of all the so-called "mountain men" of Alberta, perhaps the best-known was Justin James McCartney Simpson. But when they named a mountain after him in 1974, it became just plain Mount Jimmy Simpson.

He came from England when he was 18. That was in 1896, when no superhighways cut through the rugged Rocky Mountains. A C.P.R. conductor found him sleeping aboard his train with no ticket, and put him off at Lake Louise. Jimmy promptly got a job as a railway section hand. Later he went to the West Coast and signed on with a seal-hunting crew. One morning he overslept and missed his boat. The crew was arrested by the Russians for poaching and Jimmy missed a sentence of exile to Siberia. He also missed a prison term when he turned down an invitation to join the train-robbing gang led by Bill Miller.

Jimmy Simpson returned to the mountains, where he made his life for over 70 years. He became one of the most popular guides in the area and called his clients "pilgrims." They included such people as American humourist Will Rogers, singer-actor Burl Ives, novelist Jack London and hockey commentator Foster Hewitt. "Some of them took to the wilds like fish

57

take to water," he said. "Others should have stayed home."

One of Jimmy Simpson's main concerns was the precious water resources of the mountain glaciers. He predicted that Albertans could be forced to buy drinking water by the bottle in the next century if they didn't preserve it now. "The ordinary person is not paying enough attention to tomorrow," he complained.

Another concern was the "softness" of modern life. "People don't want to go anywhere today unless there's a good road and they can take their car."

Jimmy Simpson wasn't soft. He once hiked 74 miles by snowshoe to spend Christmas with his friend Tom Wilson, the famous guide who had discovered Lake Louise. The next day he turned around and hiked back. On the way he cheated death three times.

The first was when he broke through the ice of the North Saskatchewan River. Then he was caught in a small avalanche. Later, at his camp, he realized just in time that the white powder dropping into his frying pan wasn't snow. It was strychnine poison which he carried to bait fox traps.

In the 1920s Jimmy Simpson built a lodge called Num-Ti-Jah at Bow Lake, north of Lake Louise. Thousands of summer visitors came to appreciate this small, wiry "mountain man" with his glacier-blue eyes, his storyteller's wit and his ever-present Mountie-style hat.

Stoney Indians called Jimmy Simpson *Nashan-esen* because of his speed on snowshoes. The name means "wolverine-go-quick."

Until his death in 1972 Simpson maintained a keen interest in literature and opera. He could speak with anyone on almost any topic. At 83 he took up the hobby of watercolour painting.

Above all, though, Jimmy Simpson was a man of the mountains who respected the lesson of the outdoors: "If you listen, the wilderness teaches you. If you don't, it can kill you."

W.R. "Wop" May

They really were "magnificent men in their flying machines." The bush pilots who opened up Canada's North were pioneers, daredevils and, in a sense, nation-builders.

Among the greatest was "Wop" May. He was also "one of the finest natural flyers in the history of aviation."

Wilfred Reid May was born in Carberry, Manitoba, in 1896 but came to Edmonton at the age of six. When he died 50 years later he left a remarkable string of accomplishments behind him.

As a young pilot in the First World War he made his first combat flight on April 21, 1918 in a Sopwith "Camel." That flight made history. He was chased by Baron Manfred Von Richtofen, the German ace known as the "Red Knight." May's guns jammed, but he outmanoeuvred Richtofen for miles. Finally the German plane was shot down by another Canadian, Captain Roy Brown, a former schoolmate of "Wop" May's in Edmonton. May returned from the war with less than a year of combat experience. Yet he was given credit for shooting down 13 enemy planes and received the Distinguished Flying Cross.

Commercial aviation was still in its infancy when he got back. His pilot's licence was only the seventh issued in Canada. He and his brother, Court, formed Edmonton's first air service. Their plane, the *City of Edmonton*, was a Curtiss "Jenny" owned by the city. For some time "Wop" May made his living "barnstorming" – taking curious passengers on short flights for a fee. To the thrill of first flight was added the honour of riding with a genuine war "ace."

Pilots of the 1920s were often their own mechanics, especially on flights to remote areas. Once, after being stranded near Whitecourt, May used bacon rind and friction tape to repair a leaky radiator hose.

1929 was a banner year for "Wop" May. It began with a mercy flight to Fort Vermilion. The community was threatened by a diphtheria epidemic. May and his co-pilot, Vic Horner, set out on the 500-mile flight to deliver the needed antitoxin on January 3. Their plane had open cockpits and was equipped with wheels rather than skis. The temperature was well below zero. To keep the antitoxin from freezing they used charcoal burners during the flight.

The mission was a success. Severely wind-chilled, the two men returned to Edmonton as heroes.

Later that year May became the first person to fly to the Arctic Ocean in winter. That air mail flight to Aklavik was one of many pioneering mail runs into the Far North. In 1930 "Wop" received the McKee Trophy for "the most meritorious service for the advancement of Canadian aviation."

In 1932 he had a ringside seat for another drama that made headlines around the world. He assisted the RCMP in their search for Albert Johnson, the "Mad Trapper of Rat River." May was there when the chase across the Arctic ended in the deranged killer's death on February 17. It was the first time an aircraft had been used in a Canadian manhunt.

Wilfred R. May was created an Officer of the Order of the British Empire in 1935. That honour was chiefly for the 1929 mercy flight – just one of his pioneering experiences.

In World War II May served as supervisor of training for Canadian pilots. His development of a "search and rescue" service for airmen earned him the "Bronze Pal" – the American Medal of Freedom given by the U.S. government.

When he was inducted into the Canadian Aviation Hall of Fame in 1973, he was remembered for his "aeronautical brilliance in the cruelest geographic arenas, his total dedication to the cause of uniting people through air transport..."

Even Baron Von Richtofen would have admired him.

Louise McKinney

Alberta women gained the right to vote in 1916. Just one year later, Roberta MacAdam and Louise McKinney became the first women ever elected to a legislature in the British Empire. The first to take office was Louise McKinney.

She was born Louise Crummy in Frankville, Ontario, one of ten children of Irish immigrants. Throughout her life she called herself a "home woman" whose public activities in the temperance movement, in politics and in church work remained secondary.

Louise McKinney was, however, an outspoken supporter of women's rights. "Even as a child," she said, "I recognized and resented the disabilities laid upon women." Although she had wanted to become a doctor, she settled for the life of a schoolteacher. While teaching in North Dakota she met James McKinney, who shared her deep concern about the harmful effects of alcohol and tobacco. They were married in 1896 and moved to Claresholm, Alberta, seven years later. In 1917 Louise McKinney was elected to the Alberta legislature as a candidate for the Non-Partisan League.

Four years later the United Farmers of Alberta swept into power and she was defeated by 45 votes. In the meantime she had supported  aid for immigrants and the retarded, and for widows and deserted wives. She had spoken out for strict enforcement of liquor control laws. With Henrietta Muir Edwards, she had drafted a *Dower Act* which guaranteed Alberta widows a part of their husbands' estates.

Perhaps the high point of Louise McKinney's public career came in 1928, when she was one of five women to petition Ottawa for a ruling on the question of women being qualified to sit in the Canadian Senate. It became known as the "Persons Case." The Supreme Court of Canada ruled that, under the British North America Act, women were not "eligible persons" for Senate appointment. A year later the British Privy Council overturned that decision in one of the most important legal rulings in Canadian history.

As a new M.L.A. Louise McKinney had been the object of much scorn when she tried to prevent tobacco rations being sent to Canadians fighting in the First World War. Still, she never gave up her battle against tobacco and alcohol. For over 20 years she was both Alberta president and Dominion vice-president of the Women's Christian Temperance Union.

She also made her mark as a church worker. In 1925 she became the only woman to sign the "Basis of Union" which created the United Church of Canada.

1930 - 1938

The Lean Years

A decade of prosperity and social innovation left Albertans unprepared for the lean years that followed. Drought at home and a world-wide economic depression drove the province into new political directions. The "Great Depression" was to shape the mentality of a generation and leave an enduring scar on the political memory of a province.

R.B.
Bennett

Two Canadian prime ministers have come from Alberta. Both were Conservatives, but that is where the resemblance ends (see also Joe Clark, page 167).

The first was Richard Bedford Bennett, a wealthy, aristocratic, bachelor lawyer. He was born in Hopewell Cape, New Brunswick and died in Mickleham, England. Although he represented Calgary in the House of Commons for two decades, he "never really became a westerner," according to one biographer.

R.B. Bennett, as he was invariably known, came to Calgary in 1897 as law partner of Senator James Lougheed. Before entering law he had taught school. At the age of 18 he was principal of four schools with 140 students — for $500 a year!

His association with Sen. Lougheed made him a rich man. His own drive and ability earned him widespread respect as a corporate lawyer in both Canada and England.

Even before coming to Calgary he had been involved in politics as an alderman in Chatham, N.B. His campaign had been run by a lifelong friend, Max Aitken, who later became Lord Beaverbrook.

Before he was 20, Bennett had declared that he would be prime minister one day. After less than two years in the West he won a seat in the Territorial Assembly. He lost by only 29 votes when he ran for Alberta's first provincial legislature in 1905.

In 1909 he was successful, but he stayed in provincial politics for only two years before going to the House of Commons. In 1914 he opposed his party leader, Robert Borden, over a railway agreement, so he did not contest the 1917 election.

Between 1917 and 1925 he was often in England arguing cases before the British Privy Council. The Lougheed-Bennett partnership fell apart during this period, but R.B. Bennett also made his second fortune. He inherited the pulp and paper empire of a childhood friend, Jennie Shirreff Eddy.

He returned to parliament in 1925 and served as Minister of Justice in Arthur Meighen's three-month government of 1926. The following year he succeeded Meighen as Conservative leader. In 1930, with the Great Depression underway, his party swept William Lyon Mackenzie King's Liberals out of office with a promise to "blast a way into the markets of the world."

Five years later Mackenzie King, also a wealthy bachelor, swept back in with the slogan "King or Chaos."

One achievement of the Bennett era which survives is the Canadian Broadcasting Corporation. In its last months his government also introduced several measures to tackle Depression problems. These included unemployment insurance, farm credit, minimum wage laws, agricultural marketing boards and restrictions on unfair trade practices (later declared unconstitutional).

R.B. Bennett's own efforts also expanded Canada's markets within the British Empire and laid the foundation for both the St. Lawrence Seaway and the Reciprocity Treaty with the U.S.

Perhaps no prime minister could have done much to cure the Depression. Many historians, though, feel that what R.B. Bennett did was too little and too late. He had poured millions of dollars into relief projects and had set up labour camps for the unemployed. However, he had infuriated those same unemployed by imprisoning some of their leaders who were Communists.

He had also infuriated his own cabinet ministers by not consulting them on decisions. Several did not seek re-election or, like H.H. Stevens, ran against the Conservatives in 1935.

R.B. Bennett left Canada in 1939 to live next door to Lord Beaverbrook in England. He died there in 1947 at age 76. However, he died as "Viscount Bennett of Mickleham, Calgary, and Hopewell."

King George had granted him a peerage in 1941.

Today his name is honoured through such memorials as Viscount Bennett School in Calgary. But it has also been immortalized through a strange vehicle of the Depression period: a horsedrawn motor car with its engine removed, nicknamed the "Bennett Buggy."

Pat Burns

If any Canadian ever deserved the title of Cattle King, it was Patrick Burns. From his home south of Calgary he built up one of the world's biggest meat-packing businesses. And it all started with two oxen.

As a young man Pat Burns (or "Byrne," as the family name was then spelled) was working in the woods of northern Ontario. When his

employer couldn't pay the $100 in wages he had earned, Pat settled for a yoke of oxen. On the hoof, they were worth $70, but by slaughtering them and selling the meat, he made $140. That was in 1878. Fifty years later he sold his interest in P. Burns and Co. Ltd. for $15 million! Pat Burns was born in Oshawa, Ontario, one of ten children of Irish immigrants (whose name had been "O'Byrne" in the old country). When he was 22 he and one of his brothers struck out for the frontier province of Manitoba. There he worked as a farm-hand and later became a homesteader who dabbled in cattle dealing and supplying beef to railroad crews as far away as the State of Maine.

He was quick to recognize the business potential of the railroad. Five carloads of hogs he sent from Manitoba to Ontario comprised the first shipment of western livestock to eastern Canadian markets.

In 1890, with a growing reputation as a cattle dealer and meat

66

supplier, Pat Burns headed west again. He settled near Calgary and the building of the Burns meat-packing empire began in earnest. That first year he started a small slaughterhouse in Calgary. He shipped cattle into the Crow's Nest Pass area, to the Kootenays and farther into the British Columbia interior. The Dominion government also awarded him a contract to supply meat to the Blood Indians at Sarcee.

With his brother, Dominic, he began shipping meat to the Yukon, establishing depots and retail stores along the way. Then the expansion turned eastward again. Packing plants were built in Regina, Prince Albert and Winnipeg to go along with those in Calgary, Edmonton, Vancouver and Seattle.

Eventually the Burns interests expanded to Montreal and Great Britain, and there was even a Burns representative in Japan. Yet Pat Burns had never received much schooling, and many of his deals were made with little more than a handshake and a few notes scribbled on the back of an envelope.

One writer described Pat Burns as "small, round, pink and white." Yet he was rugged enough for the unsettled prairie, where enormous cattle herds ranged winter and summer over unfenced land. The man they called the "Cattle King of the West" also had a big heart.

Once, when he was having the small Catholic church at Midnapore painted, he instructed the crew to spruce up the neighbouring Anglican church as well. With the other members of the "Big Four" of Alberta cattle-raising, he put up the money to launch the Calgary Stampede.

Among his legions of friends were the legendary Father Albert Lacombe and Prime Minister R.B. Bennett. Although Burns was a Liberal, the Conservative prime minister named him to the Senate in 1931. Earlier he had turned down both a Senate appointment and a knighthood to concentrate on business. The appointment he did accept was announced on his 75th birthday.

The party that day was one of Canada's most gala functions ever. The City of Calgary proclaimed July 6 to 11 as "Burns Week." The Calgary Stampede hosted the party. Among the dignitaries were the prime minister, two premiers, two lieutenant-governors and two railway presidents. A "Cake for a King" which weighed 3,000 pounds was displayed and distributed. The city prepared an illuminated plaque which read, in part: "Western hospitality has been defined and crystallized in your genial personality; private benevolence has received its greatest encouragement from your unselfish liberality." Pat Burns responded to these tributes by donating 2,000 beef roasts to needy families and 2,000 meal vouchers to single unemployed men.

William Irvine

Alberta politics has seldom followed the Canadian pattern. Much of the difference came from the Progressive Movement which was a source for two existing national parties. They are Social Credit and the New Democratic Party (which grew out of the Co-operative Commonwealth Federation).

One of the midwives at the birth of the CCF in 1932 was William Irvine, a Calgary clergyman born in the Shetland Islands. This "political evangelist" had been lured to Canada in 1908 by the missionary father of James S. Woodsworth, another clergyman who later became leader of the CCF. Bill Irvine was a Presbyterian, but switched to the Methodist church to get permission to marry while still a divinity student. As a student minister he worked in the lumber camps of northern Manitoba. After ordination, his rather unorthodox views resulted in a charge of heresy. Although he was acquitted he felt stifled by the Methodist church. He accepted a position in Calgary as a Unitarian minister. Here he had the freedom to engage in political activity.

Irvine edited a newspaper called *The Nutcracker*. When he joined the farmers' political action group known as the Non-Partisan League in 1917 the paper was renamed the *Alberta Non-Partisan*. Two years later the league joined the United Farmers of Alberta, which formed the provincial government from 1921 to 1935. Eventually, Irvine's paper became the *Western Independent*.

In 1921 he was elected as a Labour member of the House of Commons representing Calgary. The only other labourite elected that year was the Rev. J.S. Woodsworth. Irvine told the Commons, "The

68

Hon. Member for Central Winnipeg, Mr. Woodsworth, is the leader of the labour group – and I am the group."

Irvine was defeated in 1925, but was re-elected the next year as a UFA candidate in Wetaskiwin. He became part of the "Ginger Group" within the Progressive Party which founded the CCF.

As a parliamentarian he was described by D. Walter Thomson in the *Edmonton Journal* in 1931: "Robust and aggressive in debate, he stands erect with his raven-haired head thrown well back and in a dry, humorous way flings broadcast his wordy stones and arrows of satiric logic."

He was defeated again in 1935 and spent the next nine years on his farm in Wetaskiwin. But he was re-elected in 1945, this time as CCF member for Cariboo in British Columbia. In 1949 he retired to Wetaskiwin.

William Irvine's political views were considered by some to be as unorthodox as his religious views. In 1923 he had been instrumental in bringing Major Clifford H. Douglas to explain his Social Credit theory to the Commons banking committee. Irvine, however, could never buy the Alberta brand of Social Credit advanced by Premier William Aberhart.

Throughout his political career, Irvine also opposed what he felt was an anti-democratic tendency in the Canadian parliamentary system. He wrote several books and two plays with socialist themes. In 1956 he visited the Soviet Union and in 1960 he travelled to China. He returned with praise for the Chinese political system.

When he died in 1962 the *Lethbridge Herald* concluded an editorial tribute with these words: "No other eulogy is needed, really, and it is probable that no other would have pleased Irvine himself so greatly: he was a member of the Ginger Group."

Elizabeth Sterling Haynes

Live theatre in Alberta owes more to Elizabeth Sterling Haynes than to any other person. In fact she has been called "the spirit mother of theatre in Alberta." For 32 years this tall, energetic actress-director coaxed theatre companies into existence and travelled the province introducing people to a new outlet for their creativity.

Although she was born in England, Elizabeth Sterling was educated in Ontario. At the University of Toronto she made her mark as a gifted actress. In 1923 she came to Edmonton with her dentist husband, Dr. Nelson Haynes.

A chance encounter with a former U. of T. professor on an Edmonton street corner led to her first directing assignment here. It was the University of Alberta production of "Dear Brutus."

In 1928 she helped establish the Alberta Drama League. Five  years later she was appointed provincial drama director for the University of Alberta's extension department. Mile after gruelling mile she would travel around Alberta by train, bus and car. Some years she logged as many as 20,000 miles. Every place she visited, people flocked to hear her talk about stagecraft and production techniques, and to ask her advice about how to develop live theatre in their communities.

A crazy dream began to come true in 1934, when the Banff School of the Theatre opened. Only 25 students had been expected, but 200 showed up. Quite a handful for Mrs. Haynes and the one other instructor! That school went on to become world-famous as the Banff School of Fine Arts.

In the meantime Elizabeth Sterling Haynes applied her talents and energy to developing theatre in Edmonton as well. She was a founder of the Edmonton Little Theatre, the Women's Theatre, the Studio Theatre and the Dominion Drama Festival. "She didn't mind killing herself, or others, for theatre," said playwright Elsie Park Gowan, a friend of Mrs. Haynes.

She also chaired the drama section of Alberta's Allied Arts Council and sat on the Edmonton recreation commission. In 1945 she was elected to the Edmonton Public School Board.

Her production of "Othello" for the Studio Theatre won the Calvert Trophy at the 1953 Dominion Drama Festival. Numerous other productions she had assisted picked up various awards over the years. Her students and co-workers have made significant contributions to theatre in Alberta and elsewhere.

Elizabeth Sterling Haynes left Edmonton in 1955 and died two years later in Toronto. In a tribute years later, Dr. W.G. Hardy said, "Her influence on the artistic life of this province was pervasive and enduring." The number of theatre companies now operating in Alberta confirms that opinion.

John W. Barnett

Alberta's teachers are now part of a strong organization which bargains for their rights. That organization, the Alberta Teachers' Association, owes much of its present strength to the work of one man. John Walker Barnett championed teachers' rights in Alberta from the time he got his first teaching position in a rural schoolhouse in 1911 to his death in 1947.

Barnett was born in Grantham, Lincolnshire, England. His father was a wheelwright and a lay Methodist preacher. John went to Grantham Wesleyan School and Grantham Technical Institute. He became an apprentice teacher, and graduated from the Westminster Teacher Training College, London, in 1902. Barnett taught in England for the next nine years and became president of a branch of the National Teachers' Union. In Canada Barnett taught first at Lougheed, later at Alberta College, and at Strathcona High School. While at Strathcona he was supervisor of music for all Edmonton schools. In 1917 he became secretary of the Alberta Teachers' Association. In 1920 he went to work for the association fulltime.

Buoyed by his union experiences in England, John set out to build a strong teachers' organization in Alberta. He envisioned an organization that would raise teaching from the status of a trade to that of a true profession. This meant ensuring teachers' rights to material well-being through respectable salaries, achieved through collective bargaining. He also wanted teachers to have security of tenure, right of appeal in the case of dismissal, transfer or demotion as well as freedom from exploitation and other rights. Barnett fought for these rights with trade union tactics.

His efforts on behalf of both teacher welfare and the quality of education won him the respect of many for whom he worked. In 1931 he was elected president of the Canadian Teachers' Federation.

His formal recognition included an honorary Doctor of Laws degree from the University of Alberta. This was conferred upon him posthumously at the 1947 fall convocation.

William Aberhart

On August 23, 1935 Alberta voters made history. In record numbers, they turned out to elect the world's first government based on a strange economic theory called Social Credit. They also chose as premier a man who wasn't even a candidate in the election: William Aberhart, known by the nickname of "Bible Bill."

William Aberhart had come to Alberta in 1910 as a school-teacher from Ontario. For 20 years after 1915 he ruled with a strict hand as principal of Calgary's Crescent Heights High School. A teacher who once worked for him described him as "...a great noise and a great light. In his presence, one felt as if one were near a magnesium flare."

There was more to William Aberhart than his teacher's profession. He was also a devout Christian of fundamentalist beliefs. As a child he had imitated evangelistic preachers by pounding pine stumps in his parents' farmyard.

Between 1911 and 1925 he went from the Presbyterian Church to the Methodist, and finally to the Baptist Church. As a lay preacher at Westbourne Baptist Church in Calgary, he organized large and popular bible classes. Later he started his own religious training school, the Prophetic Bible Institute. He also discovered the power of a new invention, radio, for putting across his message. By 1935 his weekly "Back to the Bible Hour" had a radio audience of over 350,000.

In the meantime "Bible Bill" had discovered Social Credit, the economic theory of an English engineer named Major C.H. Douglas. Its principle was the creation of "new" money to combat the power of the minority which controlled the world's money system. Canada was in the middle of the Great Depression, and William Aberhart saw in Social Credit a solution to widespread poverty.

Fundamentalist religion and Social Credit money theories became mixed in his broadcasts. His Bible study classes became Social Credit study groups — 1,600 of them across Alberta. In 1935 he handpicked Social Credit candidates for every constituency in the province. On August 23 Aberhart's candidates won in 56 of the 63 ridings.

William Aberhart was a large man, over six feet tall and weighing 260 pounds. His bald head and round "pince-nez" glasses made him a favourite subject for political cartoonists. His own sense of humour sometimes fooled his opponents into underestimating the seriousness of his mission. The people of Alberta took him seriously and saw him as their spokesman against the "big money" interests of eastern Canada.

In turn bankers and businessmen detested Social Credit theories. Canadian courts outlawed various pieces of Alberta legislation. The Lieutenant-Governor considered throwing the premier out of office after Government House was closed down. Most of the press was against him.

Still, the biggest opposition came from within the ranks of the Social Credit cabinet, from "insurgents" who felt the premier wasn't doing enough to put Major Douglas' theories into practice.

Social Credit would form the government of Alberta until 1970, chiefly under William Aberhart's friend and former student, Ernest C. Manning.

"Bible Bill," however, would not live to see the end of what he had begun. He died in Vancouver in 1943. His widow insisted he be buried there, rather than in Alberta where they had been quite unhappy for years.

Charles Sherwood Noble

The hot, dry winds of southern Alberta present farmers with a serious problem. If the land is overworked and loses its moisture, the rich topsoil may simply blow away. One man, Charles Sherwood Noble, spent a long lifetime developing new farming techniques and equipment to overcome that problem.

Charles Noble was born in the United States in 1873. By the time he died 84 years later he was known as one of Canada's most outstanding agricultural conservationists.

Yet, above all, he was a farmer. In 1903 he filed on a homestead at Claresholm, opened a butcher shop and became the local dealer for Massey-Harris farm equipment. The next year he sold both shop and dealership to buy 500 acres of land from the Hudson's Bay Company.

That was the beginning. He dreamed of creating a huge "bonanza farm" like those he had seen in the U.S.A. By 1916 he was operating six farms, and the next year his land holdings went up to a massive 30,000 acres. His crops were also remarkable. In different years his yields of flax, oats and wheat had set world records. By 1922, however, a series of crop failures ended with the loss of his land to the mortgage companies. "Charlie" Noble simply started again. Eight years later he was once more considered one of Alberta's biggest and best grain growers. Still, there was the problem of those hot, dry winds. It was a problem which would become acute in the Dust Bowl days of the 1930s. This is where Charles Noble, the inventor, came in.

He had already developed the Noble Drill, a machine used for planting. He had been an early supporter of the ideas of "strip farming" and of leaving a "trash cover" of weeds and stubble to keep unplanted fields from drying out. His Noble Foundation was selling brine-treated registered seed around the world.

Then, in 1936, he developed the Noble Blade, a special plow which made him world-famous. It was a long blade which was pulled underground, cutting off the roots of weeds. It did not disturb the surface of the soil the way traditional plows did, and so the risk of water loss was lessened.

The Noble Blade became widely used in many countries, including the United States and the Soviet Union. Today it is still being manufactured at the Noble Cultivator Company in the town of Nobleford, keeping alive the name of the "Grand Old Man of Agriculture."

75

Leonard Brockington

An eloquent voice that became famous around the world was the trademark of a Welsh-born Calgary lawyer named Leonard Walter Brockington. The son of a rural schoolteacher, "Brock" taught briefly himself before coming to Canada in 1912. He had already distinguished himself as a Classics scholar at the University of Wales.

A short stint as a newspaper reporter in Edmonton earned him enough to begin studying law. In 1913 he went to work with the Calgary firm of Lougheed and Bennett. He left after a few years because he couldn't stand the junior partner, R.B. Bennett. The feeling, apparently, was mutual. All through law school he took top honours, including the gold medal of the Alberta Law Society. Later he would be named King's Counsel by both Alberta and Manitoba. In 1921 he became city solicitor for Calgary, a post he held until 1935. That year he became general counsel for the North West Grain Dealers' Association. He rapidly developed a reputation as a brilliant lawyer and an enormously popular speaker. The Toronto *Globe and Mail* called him "a veritable encyclopedia of English poetry." His wit became legend,  and Leonard Brockington stories are still being told in certain quarters.

In 1936 he was named first chairman of the Canadian Broadcasting Corporation. It was a controversial appointment, since he had no previous radio experience. One of his policies remains in effect, however: free air time for opposing views on controversial issues.

During World War II Leonard Brockington worked as special advisor to Prime Minister King. He travelled Canada, Britain, Australia and the U.S. promoting the Commonwealth war effort, particularly the role of Canada. "Our place is not where words are spoken," he said in one speech chiding the Americans for not joining the war. "Our place is where things are done."

In 1942 he was appointed advisor on Commonwealth affairs to Britain's ministry of information. His voice became one of the best-known on radio throughout the English-speaking world. He was often on the battlefronts of Europe, despite crippling arthritis which had afflicted him since his days as a young lawyer.

After the war he became a specialist in arbitrating labour disputes, including one between the U.S. government and its employees at the United Nations. He was also Rector of Queen's University from 1947 until his death in 1966.

Leonard Brockington earned scores of tributes during his lifetime. The one he cherished most was an honorary degree from the University of Wales. It was presented in 1953, the same day the new Queen Elizabeth received a similar honour.

When he accepted a Canada Council Medal in 1963 the citation called him "the greatest Canadian exponent of the art of rhetoric in our time." He had also been called "the best after-dinner speaker in Canada." In addition he was known as an adjudicator of music and drama festivals, an accomplished amateur actor and even an occasional symphony conductor!

To his vast audiences in wartime he was the "Evangelist of Empire." To the Sarcee Indians he was "Chief Yellow Head Coming-Over-The-Hill" for his shaggy mane of blond hair. To one Calgary client he was "the man who looks like Highland cattle."

Bent over from arthritis, puffing expensive cigar smoke like his good friend, Winston Churchill, "Brock" would have laughed at the comparison. The advice he often gave others was, "Never neglect the merry heart."

Georges Bugnet

The word "culture" can be used in many different senses. In the case of Georges Bugnet it sums up a long life dedicated to literature, to public service and to the development of new plant varieties.

Georges-Charles-Jules Bugnet was born in 1879 in Châlons-sur-Saône, in the French province of Burgundy. He received a classical education at the Sorbonne and the University of Dijon.

He worked as a newspaper editor in France before coming to Canada in 1904 with his young wife, Julia. He had been lured here by the prospect of making $25,000 in a few years and returning to France a wealthy man. At the age of 100 he smiled and said, "I'm still waiting to make that $25,000."

Along the way, Georges Bugnet made many things of value. Cultural value. As an author he produced several novels and volumes of poetry. Two of his novels are *Nipsya*, about a young Cree girl and the conflicts faced by Indian and halfbreed people during the Riel Rebellion, and *La Forêt*, about the hardships of life in the Canadian wilderness. A book of verse, *Voix de la Solitude*, was reissued after 40 years in 1978 to coincide with M. Bugnet's 99th birthday.

As a school trustee for 47 years he was dedicated to education. He once walked 20 miles in mud to catch a train for Edmonton to persuade Premier Aberhart to grant more money to his school district.

As a horticulturist he developed a world-famous variety of wild rose, named the *Therese Bugnet* rose after one of his ten children. This took 25 years of patient experimenting, beginning with a cross between a Siberian double wild rose and the traditional Alberta wild rose. He also introduced a hardy Russian variety of Scots pine, the Lagoda Pine, into Alberta where it has served as an excellent windrow tree.

Georges Bugnet spent most of his life on a farm in Rich Valley, northwest of Edmonton. That farm is now preserved by the provincial government as an historic site and a source of valuable Lagoda Pine seeds.

The author-educator-horticulturalist was also one of the founders of the Alberta French Canadian Association. Throughout his life his works have brought him many honours. One was the title of *Chevalier dans l'Ordre des Palmes Academiques*, presented by the French government in 1951.

In 1979 the University of Alberta conferred upon him an honorary doctorate. The special convocation, in a church in Legal, was the first the university had conducted away from its own campus.

From his wheelchair the 99-year-old man, almost blind and deaf, told the audience he had had a "magnificent" life. Then, with the serenity that comes as a full life nears its end, he compared death to a dragonfly as it sheds its casing in the sun and "emerges into a beautiful world it had not known before."

1939 - 1947

Abroad and Home

The rains came and the war in 1939. Albertans found themselves caught up in a wartime prosperity that gave them markets abroad and a direct role in North American defence. The Pacific Staging Route brought American troops and planes through Alberta and the momentum of those years continued with the first big strike in oil. Alberta was underway.

George R. Pearkes

Berkhamsted Farm, near Red Deer, was set up by an English headmaster to train British lads for prairie farming. One of its "graduates" later became an outstanding military leader, a federal cabinet minister and Lieutenant-Governor of British Columbia. George Randolph Pearkes was 18 when he arrived in 1906. He was athletic and loved the outdoors. After two years at what local residents called the "Baby Farm" he began to work for various farmers in the area. One of them introduced him to Conservative politics, which would play a major role in his later life.

George and his brother, Edward, decided to try their luck at homesteading near Rocky Mountain House. They worked hard and George took freight-hauling jobs to make ends meet. He also spent part of one year working with a Dominion Land Survey crew north of Fort McMurray. Here he developed an admiration for the men of the Royal North-West Mounted Police.

The two brothers, along with their mother and sister, decided in 1912 that they couldn't make a go of it on the farm. George enlisted in the Mounties and was posted to the Yukon.

Then, in 1914, the First World War broke out. George immediately enlisted in the 2nd Canadian Mounted Rifles. Within four years he was Lt.-Col. George R. Pearkes. He had been wounded in battle five times. One bomb had injured him in eight separate places. Also, he had earned the highest military honours in the Empire – the Victoria Cross (VC), Distinguished Service Order (DSO) and the Military Cross (MC). The French government had awarded him the *Croix de Guerre*.

82

George Pearkes remained in the army and achieved the rank of Major-General. In World War II he commanded the 1st Canadian Division overseas from 1940 to 1942. Then he was put in charge of Canada's Pacific Command. Soon after being relieved of that post in 1945 he was elected to the House of Commons as a Conservative.

He was re-elected in the elections of 1949, 1953, 1957 and 1958. George Pearkes seemed the natural choice for Minister of National Defence in the Diefenbaker government. He held the post from 1957 to 1960.

Some critics felt he was too influenced by senior military personnel and a weak salesman for Canadian military equipment. To other observers he stood out as an unconventional defence minister who wanted to eliminate inefficiency in the armed forces and who advocated Canadian recognition of the People's Republic of China.

In 1960 he was appointed Lieutenant-Governor of British Columbia, a post he held until 1968. Many consider him the most popular person ever to hold that office.

George Pearkes' attitude to public service was probably best expressed when he received the Pacific Command appointment in 1942. "I am not exactly accustomed to making pretty speeches," he told reporters. "But this you can say: I am supremely proud of the great honour that has been conferred upon me, and I pray God that I shall have the courage and good judgment to be worthy of that trust."

Wilf Carter

Long before Linda Ronstadt, Merle Haggard or Dolly Parton, there was a man called Wilf Carter. He didn't sing Country and Western. He sang "cowboy music."

Wilf Carter was a cowboy, although he was born in Nova Scotia, one of nine children of a poor Baptist minister. When he was 12 Wilf came to Alberta as a field hand and his life as a singing cowboy began.

For a time he lived in a deserted shack near Carbon, Alberta with a mongrel dog for company. He would skin coyotes for his "living money" and spend most of his time composing songs and practising the cowboy yodel that became his trademark.

That yodel had been part of him from the age of 10 when he had paid a day's wages, 25 cents, to hear a singer called "The Yodelling Fool."

As a cowboy he worked at the Calgary Stampede. One of his jobs

was "eardowning," or biting the ears of wild horses to calm them for saddling. While competing in the 1931 Stampede, Wilf began singing on a Calgary radio station for $5 a show. His show business career had started. Soon afterward he was hired by the C.P.R. to sing on trail rides and later on one of its cruise ships. One thing led to another. A demonstration record he made in Montreal was released and gained some popularity. On one side was *The Capture of Albert Johnson* and on the other was *My Swiss Moonlight Lullaby*. Both songs had been written in Alberta. By 1934 he was a star on CBS Radio, with his own daily show carried over 250 stations. He received 10,000 fan letters a week.

While he was in New York with that show he met and married a nurse named Bobbie Bryan. They bought a 320-acre cattle ranch near Calgary.

A car accident in Montana in 1940 took Wilf Carter out of the singing business for nine years. He had made so many records before that, however, that the record company just kept releasing new ones as if he were still active. Wilf Carter's singing style attracted many imitators. In the United States, where he was known as Montana Slim, some singers even used his name. But the *real* Wilf Carter was one of a kind.

He never learned to read music, but he put out hundreds of records of his own songs. He was elected to both the Nashville Country Music Hall of Fame and the National Cowboy Hall of Fame in

84

Oklahoma City.

This Nova Scotia cowboy who has lived in New Jersey and is now retired in Florida, is popular around the world. His songs are especially loved in England, France and Australia. But for the tall, smiling singer with his purple suit and white Stetson, hometown is still Calgary, Alberta.

Grant McConachie

In the early days of aviation, the canvas-covered biplanes had to be wiped down after every flight. Around Edmonton the job often went to "that freckle-faced kid who used to hang around the airport."

George William Grant McConachie didn't just hang around the airport. He lived next door. And his love of planes carried him to the top of one of the world's major airlines. Grant came to Edmonton from Ontario as a baby, but he grew into a towering man well over six feet tall. He also became a giant in the aviation industry. In 1930 the 21-year-old pilot was headed for China to fly for a small airline. An uncle talked him out of the idea by buying him a Fokker aircraft for $2,500. Independent Airways, Ltd. had begun. Chief pilot: Grant McConachie. His first cargo consisted of 800 crows, their tails painted yellow for migration experiments. Bad weather forced the plane down, and curious farmers shot the crows. Independent Airways was hardly off to a "flying start."

A crash near Edmonton in 1932 gave Grant McConachie broken ankles, kneecaps, ribs and wrists. It also gave him a

wife, Margaret MacLean, the nurse who had looked after him. In the tough tradition of bush pilots, he went back to work long before the doctors said he should, using a long-handled axe as a crutch on treacherous northern ice.

Later, with a Russion prince and princess as financial backers, he became the "Flying Fish-Packer." In 160 days he flew over a million pounds of fresh Alberta whitefish from northern lakes to the nearest rail line. From there they sped to hungry American markets.

All through the Depression years Grant McConachie went on borrowing money, investing his profits in new planes, hiring more pilots. He picked up mail contracts from the federal government; he flew over 200 "mercy" flights; he carried every kind of cargo imaginable, from sled dogs to fresh vegetables.

A network of tiny airstrips throughout Alberta, British Columbia, the Yukon and Northwest Territories was built for Grant McConachie. His name became known in every hamlet in the North.

During World War II he managed the observer school at Portage La Prairie, Manitoba. He also supervised the opening of a vital north-west air route used to supply planes from the U.S. across Siberia to the Russian allies.

In 1942 his career took a completely different course. He helped bring together several small bush air companies, including his own Yukon Southern Air Transport, into one large organization. It was bought by Canadian Pacific Railways and became CP Air. Grant McConachie became its western general manager and in 1947 was named president of the company.

Under his leadership CP Air became the seventh-largest airline in the world, sending its planes into Europe, the Orient and South America.

Until his death in 1965 Grant McConachie was known as a first-class airline administrator, at home anywhere in the world. But at heart he always remained the daring bush pilot his friends had once called "the human airplane."

Hedwig Bartling

Canadians of Japanese ancestry had a tough time during World War II. Because Canada was at war with Japan they were viewed with suspicion and contempt by many other Canadians. The federal government uprooted Japanese-Canadians living in British Columbia and moved them inland. Businesses were destroyed – even those belonging to second- and third-generation Canadian families.

Many of the West Coast evacuees were relocated in the countryside of southern Alberta, in the Lethbridge-Taber area. There they were fortunate to meet a United Church missionary who treated them  with dignity and compassion. Hedwig Dorothea Henriette Bartling understood discrimination. She had felt its sting in Saskatoon as a young girl who had recently arrived from Germany. She grew up determined to do something about it. After teacher training in Saskatchewan she taught in that province for five years. However, she felt some training in social work would permit her to serve the community better. Although she had been brought up as a Lutheran she enrolled in the United Church Training School in Toronto. She went on to take a diploma in social work at the University of Toronto. In her spare time she taught English to Hungarian immigrants.

In 1933 she was engaged by the Women's Missionary Society of her adopted church to work among the Ukrainian people of northeastern Alberta. After seven years of preaching and teaching and practical nursing she entered the University of British Columbia where she received a B.A. in history in 1942.

That was the year the Japanese-Canadians were evacuated. Hedwig Bartling went to Lethbridge under the auspices of the Southern Alberta Presbytery to work among these dislocated "Nisei" people.

She quickly gained their confidence and respect. For the rest of the wartime period she helped them adjust to their new life as dryland farmers, forbidden to live in the city. She organized camps, sporting events, dances and public speaking competitions. Her aim was to help the young people, especially, develop confidence and skills in community leadership.

These efforts frequently brought her into conflict with authority. RCMP security personnel grilled her about what she was teaching the "XBC"s (ex-British Columbians). But Hedwig Bartling was no respecter of arbitrary power. She encouraged young Nisei girls to work in the city as maids, in defiance of the regulations.

Discrimination ran high against the evacuees and against the friend they called "Barty." For some time the only accommodation she could get was a small basement suite.

After the war Hedwig Bartling quietly returned to B.C. She worked with a Chinese mission in Victoria and later with the returning Japanese evacuees. She was ordained in 1963 and worked as a minister until 1970. Even after her retirement to Vancouver she kept busy with hospital visiting and other church work.

When the University of Lethbridge granted her an honorary doctorate in 1980, the Japanese-Canadian community there remembered her affectionately. Wrote one member: "...the quality of civic responsibility exercised by the Japanese-Canadians today is due largely to the kind of treatment they received from a small minority of understanding people...I count the Rev. H.D. Bartling as foremost and most outstanding among all these."

Donald Cameron

The weed problems of central Alberta farmers led to the development of the Banff School of Fine Arts. The catalyst was Senator Donald Cameron.

As a young agriculture student at the University of Alberta Don Cameron spent his summers as a field supervisor for the provincial department of agriculture. In the summer evenings he heard farm families talk about their need for cultural activities, and the seed of a dream was sown.

Donald Cameron was born in England in 1903, the son of a British Admiralty engineer. The family moved to Hong Kong, where Donald learned to speak Chinese by the time he was three.

The promise of land and instant wealth lured the family to western Canada in 1906. Donald's father quickly became immersed in Alberta politics. He helped found the Non-Partisan League and later sat in the Alberta legislature as the United Farmers member from Innisfail from 1921 to 1935.

Donald shared his father's interests, serving as the UFA's junior president from 1921 until he went off to college in 1926. The day he graduated he was hired by the University of Alberta extension department as lecturer and agricultural secretary. In 1932 he won a Carnegie travel scholarship to the Scandinavian countries. The folk schools of Denmark particularly impressed him. What he saw stayed with him.

In 1936 Donald Cameron succeeded Dr. E.A. Corbett as director of extension and director of what had become the Banff School of Fine Arts. From then until his retirement in 1969 he spared no efforts to enrich his "Campus in the Clouds." He involved himself in every aspect of the school's growth. He designed its floor plans. With Eric Harvie he scouted out the ideal site, then coaxed the National Parks Board to let him have it. He launched exhaustive fund-raising drives, "rattling my tin cup over the highways and byways of Canada."

The school, of course, grew into one of the world's major cultural centres. In 1952 Donald Cameron also founded the Banff School of Advanced Management which has since developed an international stature of its own.

Donald Cameron earned his spurs as a superb administrator. In 1955 he was named to the Senate of Canada, but accepted that honour only after being assured he could continue his work at Banff.

In the Senate, too, Donald Cameron earned an impressive reputation, particularly as vice-chairman of the Senate Committee on Science Policy. He has been active in numerous organizations, including the Commonwealth Parliamentary Association. In 1958 he was asked to chair a provincial Royal Commission on Education. His most memorable accomplishment, though, is the flowering of a dream in the mind of a young field supervisor years ago.

Matthew Halton

August 27, 1944.
"This is Matthew Halton of the CBC speaking from Paris...I am telling you about the liberation of Paris, about our entry into Paris yesterday, and I don't know how to do it...Yesterday was the most glorious and splendid day I've ever seen."

That broadcast from the Scribe Hotel in Paris was relayed through Britain and heard across Canada. It told of the end of Nazi rule in France. And it was the finest moment in the career of Canada's finest war correspondent.

Matthew Henry Halton was born in Pincher Creek, Alberta, in 1904. He taught school near Claresholm for a brief period before earning a scholarship to the London School of Economics. After studying there and at King's College he returned to Canada in 1931 and joined the *Toronto Star*. The next year his paper sent him back to London to cover English and European politics. For eight years, as storm clouds grew over Germany, he reported the political weather of Europe.

As early as 1934 he warned that Germany was heading toward war. The year before he had been "scared out" of Germany by threats resulting from his outspoken reports. In 1940 the *Star* brought him back to North America as its Washington correspondent. He dined on sausage and eggs with President Franklin Delano Roosevelt the night he defeated Wendell Wilkie.

The war Halton had predicted was now underway. He was sent to cover the African campaign of Field Marshal Montgomery. From that experience came Halton's book, *Ten Years to Alamein*, considered among the best books to come out of World War II. Before it was published Halton was hired by the CBC as a war correspondent.

Halton's reports were those of an eyewitness – clear, often emotional, but always honest. He covered the campaign in Sicily and the D-day landing on the beaches of Normandy that led to the liberation of Paris and the eventual end of Hitler's Nazis.

After the war Matthew Halton became the CBC's chief European correspondent. He was just as comfortable interviewing world leaders as he had been speaking with foot-soldiers during the war. His conversations read like a history of 20th-Century public affairs – Winston Churchill, Albert Einstein, Charles de Gaulle, George Bernard Shaw, Dwight Eisenhower, Marshal Tito, Mahatma Gandhi, Haille Selassie, Pandit Nehru, and so on.

He had also once argued with Adolph Hitler's lieutenant, Hermann Goering, "until we were both blue in the face." That was in 1938, the year he made the first live radio report from Munich to North America.

When Matthew Halton died in 1956 he was well-remembered by the *Lethbridge Herald*, the first paper for which he had written. "He was a realist, and interpreted the European scene as he saw it and felt it," the paper's editorial stated.

Matthew Halton was a war correspondent who hated the horrors of war. His philosophy was expressed succinctly near the end of his book on the African campaign: "Idealism is the only realism."

Chester Ronning

For many Albertans, English is a second language. For Chester Ronning, it was the third.

The distinguished diplomat, author and politician was born in Fancheng, Hupeh Province, China in 1894. Hence his first language. "I spoke only Chinese at age six," he says.

His parents were Lutheran missionaries and his mother, from Norway, taught him his second language, Norwegian.

The family was forced out of China by the Boxer Rebellion of 1900 and fled to Iowa. Only then did Chester Ronning begin to speak English, and somewhat reluctantly: "I didn't like to learn a third language just to play with the other kids."

The family soon returned to China, but Chester and his brother, Nelius, emigrated to Alberta in 1907 after their mother died. For some time they homesteaded near Camrose until Chester and his brothers

moved to the Peace River country to taste the cowboy life in 1921. The next year the call of China proved too strong for Chester and he went off to study in Peking. His love affair with China and its people never ended. Although not a Communist, he admired the social experiment being conducted by Chairman Mao Tse-tung. Chester Ronning's voice was one of the first raised to urge Canada and other western nations to recognize "Red China."

In 1932, back in Canada, he was elected to the Alberta legislature for the United Farmers of Alberta party. Three years later he attempted to become the first elected member of the CCF party (which later became the New Democratic Party). He lost in the big sweep by William Aberhart's Social Credit.

Chester Ronning went on to become Alberta leader of the CCF, but it was in the diplomatic field rather than politics that he made his biggest mark.

He had fought in the First World War. In World War II he became a Squadron Leader with the RCAF in the intelligence service. At war's end he was posted to China by the Department of External Affairs, "without any training as a civil servant, or as a diplomat, and I haven't had any training since."

In 1951 he was recalled from China and three years later was appointed Canada's Ambassador to Norway and Iceland. He represented Canada at the Geneva conferences on Korea and Vietnam in 1954 and on Laos in 1961. He was also Canada's High Commissioner to India from 1957 to 1964.

Canada tried to negotiate a settlement of the Vietnam war in 1966. The country's hopes were tied up in one man: Chester Ronning, special envoy to Saigon and Hanoi. He was unable, however, to bring about peace between the United States and North Vietnam.

92

From the exciting life of international diplomacy Chester Ronning retired to the quiet country life of Camrose, Alberta. In 1980 the National Film Board of Canada released a film about Chester Ronning, entitled "China Mission." Its director, Tom Radford, summed up his subject with these words:

"This is a man whose dreams were decimated time after time. Yet each time he came back and persevered – because he never had any illusions of his own importance."

Alexander Calhoun

In 1913 the British poet Rupert Brooke made a tour of Canada. Among the things he wrote about was this country's system of public libraries. He felt they got better as one progressed westward. But the brand-new Calgary Public Library appealed to him most. "Few large English towns could show anything as good," he wrote. The credit belonged to Alexander Calhoun.

Calhoun had come to Calgary as chief librarian two years earlier. He was 31 and already had a reputation as a classical scholar. He had also set up the first public library in Fort William, Ontario. He stepped off the train on a February day in 1911. "I had come to organize a library," he wrote. "The balmy chinook was abroad in the land and the air was like wine."

Alexander Calhoun never left Calgary. When he died in 1979, just months short of his 100th birthday, he left behind a remarkable record of community service.

He was born in the Ontario sawmill village of Fenelon Falls.

Studies in Kingston, Chicago and Winnipeg gave him solid academic credentials in Greek, English literature, political science, German and French. It was while he was teaching high school in Fort William that he helped establish a public library board.

When the members of Calgary's library board hired him for $1,800 a year, they didn't know what a bargain they were getting. Calhoun quickly plunged into community activities. He persuaded the city to set aside vacant lots for gardens during the First World War, for a rental fee of $1. Immediately over 1,500 gardens sprang up.

Calhoun took a brief leave of absence from the library during 1918. He went to Vladivostock, Russia with the Canadian Expeditionary Force. "There we sat on our fannies, along with other allied forces," he said. "It was all a complete farce."

Alexander Calhoun was not one to sit on his "fanny" for long. He was a member of Calgary's first planning commission. He was a charter member of the Calgary branch of the Knights of the Round Table, one of the original directors of the Canadian Library Council and first president of the Alberta Library Association.

As a hiker, camper and mountain climber, Calhoun remained physically active for years. The day before he turned 85 he climbed Sulphur Mountain, near Banff.

His interests were always varied. He belonged to the Canadian Institute of International Affairs, the Canada Foundation and the Alpine Club. He was also president of the Alberta Society of Artists and first president of the Allied Arts Council in Calgary.

"I have no creative gifts," he said in 1969, "only an interest in the arts because they have an important role to play in any community."

He *did* organize that library, by the way. As Calgary's Chief Librarian for 34 years he created an impressive library system which emphasized selection and training of staff. He also believed in getting books into circulation, not stored away in "rare book" rooms.

His respect for the "common man" had been deepened in the summer of 1900 when he worked in northern Saskatchewan with a survey party. That respect included the "common woman" as well. In 1916 he joined the fight to win Alberta women the right to vote.

"All my life," he said much later, "I have fought for the underdog."

94

Illingworth Kerr

Illingworth Kerr is one of Canada's foremost painters of animals and landscapes. As a teacher and painter he also had a great deal of influence on many artists of Alberta.

Kerr was born in 1905 in Lumsden, Sask. He began drawing animals as a very young boy, encouraged by his mother, an amateur water colourist. Immediately after high school in 1924 he spent a summer as a dump wagon driver. This job gave him both the nickname 'Buck' and the $100 that took him to Toronto. Here he took an art course at the Central Technical School. Financed by a generous uncle, Kerr went on to four years' study at the Ontario College of Art (1924 - 1927). Arthur Lismer, J.E.H. MacDonald, F.H. Varley and J.W. Beatty all taught Illingworth, although none of them specifically taught the Group of Seven's approach to rendering landscapes. In the same year he visited the studios of Lawren Harris and A.Y. Jackson. But despite his four years of art college, Kerr considers himself basically self-taught.

He returned to Lumsden in 1927 where he painted and earned his living as a farm hand, a sign writer, a hunter and a trapper. His canvasses were based on the sketches he did in the field.

Illingworth Kerr also proved an accomplished writer. He began to write stories of adventure and humour. His *Gay Dogs and Dark Horse* was to be published in 1946 with his own illustrations.

Kerr's experiences and adventures provided grist for the mill of his writing and painting talents. His relationship with nature found expression in both paint and print.

1936 found him with enough money and incentive to carry him to England, where he worked on documentary films and studied at the

Westminster School of Art in London. In Scotland he wrote Canadian stories for *Blackwood's* Magazine. Over the next few years Kerr created his four dioramas for the Canadian Government display in the Empire Exhibition at Glasgow. He and his new wife travelled Europe. They returned to Canada in 1939.

Kerr's early work now seems representational. But after 1955, and a summer school at Hans Hoffmann School of Fine Art in Princetown, Mass., his work took a turn toward the abstract. He became interested in the works of Marc Chagall, Picasso, Braque and in totem art. As Kerr says, "art feeds on art." But he was still grappling with the particular problems of painting prairie landscapes.

Kerr taught for several years, and headed the Alberta College of Art from 1947 to 1967. His influence created one of the most respected art schools in Canada. Kerr's accolades are many and include an honorary PhD from the University of Calgary.

But an artist's worth and genius are to be found finally in his work, not in his biographies. Kerr's paintings can be found in many of the major art museums and galleries across Canada.

98 – W.O. Mitchell of Calgary, major Candian writer renowned for his prairie novels including "Who Has Seen the Wind?"

99 – Lawrence Grassi of Canmore, mountaineer, humanitarian and trailmaker. Lone builder of trails and rescuer of mountain climbers in the Banff-Lake Louise region.

100 – A.E. Cross, one of the "Big Four" of Alberta cattle ranching. He helped establish the Calgary Stampede in 1912.

101 – Karl Clark, scientist and innovator who devoted his career to solving the problems of the Northern Alberta tar sands.

102 – Mary Schaffer, naturalist and illustrator whose early books on the flora of the Rocky Mountains introduced the Alberta wilderness to an international readership.

103 – Henry Wise Wood, founder of the United Farmers of Alberta and a principal figure in the development of the Alberta Wheat Pool.

104 – Marion and Jim Nicoll, prominent artists of Calgary. Using separate styles of painting both husband and wife are recognized among Canada's significant painters.

105 – Crowfoot, Alberta's most prominent Indian chief. A friend of Father Lacombe, he used his influence to prevent a bloody war with white settlers during the North-West Rebellion.

106 – John McDougall, early Methodist missionary who recorded his travels throughout Alberta in a series of published journals.

107 – J. Frank Moodie, early Drumheller coal mine developer and devoted collector of birds, animals and geological specimens.

108 – John Charyk, beloved schoolteacher in Hanna and other rural communities in central Alberta. He recorded the sounds of a prairie town from grasshoppers to telegraph keys.

109 – W.R. "Wop" May, northern Alberta's most romantic bush pilot. His exploits on rescue missions made him famous throughout the North.

110 – Bob Edwards, legendary Calgary newspaperman and publisher of the "Eye Opener" the little newspaper with the biggest circulation west of Winnipeg.

111 – Lee Alward, Peace River farmer and oil entrepreneur. Made a fortune from natural gas after a life-long quest in petroleum prospecting.

112 – J.W. Grant MacEwan, historian, educator and conservationist, he became one of Alberta's most popular Lieutenat-Governors.

Paintings by Don Inman, courtesy of Suncor Inc.

LEE ALWARD

GRANT MacEWAN

1948 - 1960

The Bumper Crop

The farm base which had sustained Albertans through prosperity and depression was now only one option among many. A reverse migration into the cities changed the rural character of Alberta within a decade and signalled new economic patterns. The migration was also to stretch the social fabric of a province.

W.G. Hardy

Alberta's universities have been home to many remarkable personalities. Among the most prominent was William George Hardy, classics scholar, historian, author and hockey executive. He was possibly the most popular lecturer the U. of A. ever had.

An Ontario farm hardly seems the ideal breeding ground for a Greek and Latin scholar. But it was while ploughing his father's fields that W.G. Hardy taught him-self the Greek language. "You just buy the books," he said. He had already learned Latin, had finished public school by the age of ten, and "...used to write long, epic poems when I was 12." Throughout his 84-year life Hardy remained an ardent scholar. His normal reading speed was 300 pages an hour, with full comprehension. As a writer he was equally fast. A short story he wrote in 1945 took him 25 minutes and earn-ed $200; one of his best novels, *City of Libertines*, was also completed in record time.

There is no disputing Har-dy's academic credentials. He graduated from the University of Toronto in 1917, capturing medals in Classics and English as well as the Governor-General's gold medal as the university's top student.

Sports were always impor-tant to George Hardy. Later in life he was president of both the Canadian Amateur Hockey Association and the International Hockey Association. He was also inducted into the Edmonton Sports Hall of Fame. Why combine sports with scholarship? "That was the Greek way of doing things," he explained. "I didn't want to become a straight academic. I was too interested in people."

114

While lecturing in Classics at the University of Toronto he polished off a Masters degree in 1919. Three years later he received a doctorate in Greek and Roman literature from the University of Chicago. That year he became an assistant professor at the U. of A. From 1938 to 1964 he headed the Classics department of the Edmonton university.

Despite the demands of scholarship, W.G. Hardy was a prolific writer. His first novel, *Son of Eli*, was serialized in *Maclean's Magazine* in 1928. It was followed by over 200 short stories and half a dozen novels, many based on Greek and Roman historical topics.

Hardy also wrote a major Canadian history book, *From Sea Unto Sea*, and was editor-in-chief for both the *Alberta Golden Jubilee Anthology* in 1955 and *Alberta: A Natural History* in 1967. He served three terms as president of the Canadian Authors Association.

This output was possible because of Hardy's high energy and the discipline to meet a set quota of words every day. "I write very fast," he said. "I never pretended to be a genius, but I have a talent for writing. I know my stuff."

That statement was made in 1979, just months before Hardy's death at the age of 84. He had just finished the manuscript of a new historical novel, *The Bloodied Toga*, the second part of a fictional version of Julius Caesar's life.

Dr. Hardy earned many awards during his lifetime. Probably because – as he said of his brief public school career – "they just let me go at my own speed."

Clifford E. Lee

To some people a millionaire socialist might seem out of place in Alberta. Yet Clifford E. Lee was thoroughly Albertan. A month after the province came into being he was born on a farm which is now part of Edmonton's Hardisty district.

He was first a teacher and later a pharmacist, but it was the house-building industry that made him a wealthy man.

Clifford Lee graduated from the Camrose Normal School in 1924. For ten years he taught in country schools. He also apprenticed with a pharmacist in Ryley for two years and decided to seek a degree in Pharmacy from the University of Alberta.

Early in life Clifford Lee had developed a keen interest in politics. He had been a member of the Tuxis Boys' Parliament. But the U. of A. in the early 1930s didn't allow political activity on campus. Lee soon

became part of an off-campus group of the new CCF. That was the left-wing party which designed the Regina Manifesto of 1933. It later became the New Democratic Party. When the CCF newspaper, *People's Weekly*, began under the editorship of Elmer Roper (who became a mayor of Edmonton), Clifford Lee was one of its regular columnists. Later he would serve several terms as Alberta president of the CCF. He would also run unsuccessfully for the party both federally and provincially.

In the meantime his pharmacy business in downtown Edmonton was flourishing. But Clifford Lee wasn't a typical free-enterprise pharmacist. He encouraged the people who worked for him to buy shares and become partners in his business. He also started Edmonton's first grocery co-operative, although it failed to take root.

The turning point for Clifford Lee came in 1945. As servicemen returned from World War II, Alberta experienced a housing shortage. Lee became interested in finding a way to provide housing at a reasonable price for those who needed it. Although he had no experience in house-building, he was a skilled businessman. Using the same principle of partner-managers, he attracted other talented persons to work with him.

One such person was Ralph Scurfield. Lee took him on to manage a housing project in Thompson, Manitoba. Scurfield went on to head Nu West Homes, a small company Lee started in the booming city of Calgary. Nu West prospered. It became one of the biggest housing development companies in North America. When it became a public corporation in the late 1960s Clifford E. Lee was suddenly wealthy.

It had never been Lee's purpose to make big money from housing. Accordingly, the bulk of his profits was turned into a charitable

116

foundation, the Clifford E. Lee Foundation. Over the years it has made substantial contributions to projects in the performing arts, social services, wildlife conservation, native concerns and international relief.

The man whose business acumen and humanitarian principles spawned this charity did not live to see his generosity bear its full fruit. Clifford E. Lee died in 1972, just three years after the foundation was established.

Laura Attrux

When Laura Attrux received an honorary doctorate from the University of Alberta in 1970 she gave some advice to the nursing graduates of that year. "Above all, become involved with people – make friends, they are your most treasured asset."

Hundreds of letters from people in northern Alberta had flooded the university in support of her nomination for the degree. All were from friends she had found in her 35 years of outpost medical service.

But Laura Attrux felt as if she didn't have a friend in the world when she arrived at her first government posting in Valleyview, Alberta, in 1939. After living in cities such as Toronto and Calgary for 12 years, she was stricken with doubt when she surveyed that isolated community.

The landscape was a sea of mud surrounding a pitiful huddle of shacks – one of them a small store and post office, another a small cafe, and a gas station. One of the community's three farm trucks grunted through the mud track that masqueraded as main street. A group of children, looking like tattered scarecrows in cast-off clothes, surrounded her in grimy-faced curiosity.

But Laura squared her shoulders, told herself "you're not a quitter," and marched through the door of the tiny cottage provided for her by the townspeople.

As an outpost nurse, Laura was expected to treat diseases, attend to accident injuries, provide maternity care and carry out public health work such as health education, clinics and immunization.

"But we did more than that," she says. "We had to. There were no veterinarians, so we assumed that role as well, treating everything from canaries to Clydesdale horses." She was also a dentist, counsellor, social worker and community leader.

Transportation, or the lack of it, proved to be the biggest obstacle to the performance of her duties. Being resourceful, she concocted

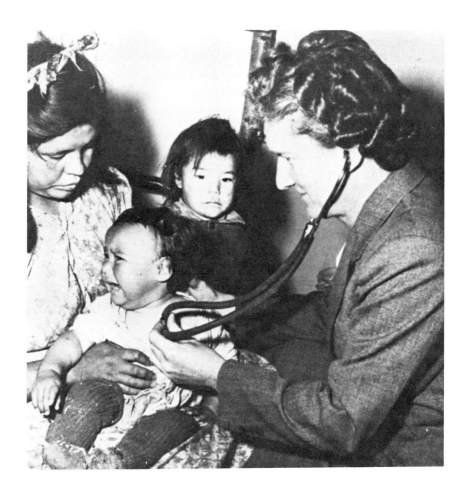

several ingenious methods of reaching her outpatients or moving the patients to a doctor or hospital. Dog teams, horses, snowshoes, skis, even a team of oxen were used in emergencies. Usually a sturdy pair of feet took her the usual two or three miles between house calls.

Laura Attrux stuck it out for two years in Valleyview, taking her services to the district homesteaders, most of them farmers who had fled Saskatchewan's dust bowl. She learned to love the country, the people, the satisfaction of her work, the sunny summers and the winter snow (but never the mud) before she moved on to a new posting at Whitecourt.

She didn't stop there either. Before Laura Attrux retired in 1974, she served the communities of Smith, Slave Lake, Wabasca, Swan Hills, Paddle Prairie, High Level and the vast regions surrounding these centres.

Laura, now over 70, is quick to point out that she was only one of hundreds of nurses who have served the isolated communities of Alberta since the beginning of the Department of Public Health's district nursing division in 1919.

But unlike many others, Dr. Attrux devoted most of her life to her outpost career. Beginning it at a time when snowshoes were a major means of transportation in the wilderness and ending it at the controls of her own Cessna 150 bush plane, she managed to bridge the gap between yesterday and today. She also never forgot her "most treasured asset."

Mary Percy Jackson

"The ability to ride a horse would be an advantage" was the line that caught and held Dr. Mary Percy's attention. Part of an ad run in 1929 seeking British doctors to work in northern Alberta, it stirred her imagination because she loved horses but rarely had the time to ride them. Understandably so. By the time she was 24, Mary Percy had graduated from the University of Birmingham with four medical degrees, a Queen's scholarship, and had worked as a house physician and house surgeon in Birmingham General Hospital.

Snared by the horses and the promise of a romantic adventure in Canada's "wild west," the prim and proper young doctor set sail for Canada in June, 1929. A month

119

later she travelled one hundred miles north of Peace River on a river barge.

When the barge landed, Mary embarked with her 29 pieces of luggage on a bone-shaking eleven-hour wagon ride. The temperature was 95 degrees F. and the air thick with mosquitoes.

If any romantic notions survived her journey, they died as soon as she saw the fourteen-by-twenty shack that was to be her hospital and her home.

Gone were the clean, well-equipped hospitals she was used to; gone were any traces of the comforts a civilized city offers.

Mary's employer, the Alberta government, had assigned her a territory of roughly 350 square miles. They had equipped her shack with basic medical supplies. There was no running water or electricity. The nearest medical aid was in Peace River, 75 miles away by dirt road.

Her only means of transportation was a saddle horse, but she had come prepared for that – or so she thought.

Her first house calls were made in proper British riding clothes; breeches, boots and a riding habit. After an average 20 miles a day she couldn't pull the boots from her swollen feet. Eventually moccasins and a buckskin jacket replaced the formal attire.

She delivered hundreds of babies in one-room shacks and in smoky tents; performed operations by candlelight on kitchen tables, battled tuberculosis and rabies, pulled teeth and even treated livestock.

Despite the hardships, Dr. Percy fell in love with northern Alberta and its people.

In 1930 she married Frank Jackson, a farmer and rancher who shared her enthusiasm for the land. They moved further north to Keg River.

Here, though no longer under contract with the government, she continued practising medicine because "when people were ill I couldn't refuse them." She was paid for her services in blueberries, moccasins, or moosemeat as none of her patients could pay cash. In fact, she received no regular pay for her work until the introduction of medicare in the 1960s.

Mary's practice in the Keg River area continued until her retirement in 1974. Somewhere in those hectic years she also managed to become an author, raise five children and take an active part in improving the standard of education in her community.

Over the years Dr. Jackson received many awards, including the Centennial Medal of Canada and the Alberta Achievement Award. The school near Keg River was named in her honour.

Earle Parkhill Scarlett

Dr. Earle Parkhill Scarlett once said, "Experience has taught us that it is the *uncommon* people – those with more character, more thought, more imagination and more understanding – that really guide the world."

Dr. Scarlett should know. In all the things he has done in his life – messenger boy, store clerk, sleeping car conductor, soldier, teacher, doctor, author, scholar, university chancellor – he remained an uncommon man.

Earle Scarlett's life began in 1896 in the hamlet of High Bluff, Manitoba. He shared the wandering life of a Methodist minister with his parents until he turned 15, when he became a nomad on his own. His father told him that his income, education and future were all up to him from that day onward.

Earle knew nothing about his future. Medicine was far from his thoughts. Deciding on an arts degree from the University of Manitoba, he supported himself with odd jobs until his graduation in 1916.

The First World War consumed him after he graduated and he spent two years fighting overseas. Severely wounded in 1918, he spent the seven months before his release in hospitals.

When Earle returned home he began to consider medicine as a career. In a quiet survey of his father's friends he found that the only men who were content with their lives were the doctors.

His career decision felt right and he entered the University of Toronto faculty of medicine. While there he became founder and editor of North America's first undergraduate medical journal. In his spare time he became distracted by a pretty young arts graduate, Jean Odell, and married her after graduating in 1924.

121

After an internship in the United States Dr. Scarlett moved to Calgary where he joined the Associate Clinic and made a home for his wife and three children.

"Those were the days," he says, looking back to 1930, "when doctors cured typhoid by immersing the patient in a tub of water with ice floating in it – to bring the fever down."

Aware that there was no one documenting medical pioneering in Alberta, Dr. Scarlett began the *Calgary Associate Historical Bulletin*, which successfully recorded the now obsolete practices of that era.

The same year the *Bulletin* began, Dr. Scarlett began giving sex education classes at the YMCA. In 1931, this caused a furor of opposition – including complaints to the police.

Earle Scarlett's life may have been controversial, but it was never dull. He attended the Baker Street Irregulars – a society devoted to the study of Sherlock Holmes.

He also fought for survival of the arts in education through his role as Chancellor of the University of Alberta. He did the things he believed in.

Raymond Urgel Lemieux

A small northern Alberta community may have seemed an unpromising start for an internationally-known scientist. Raymond Urgel Lemieux's career didn't seem to suffer. He is now among Canada's top scientists and one of the leading chemists of his field in the world.

Lemieux was born in Lac La Biche in 1920. In 1943 he received a Bachelor of Science degree with honours in Chemistry from the University of Alberta. A Ph.D in Chemistry from McGill University followed in 1946. Post graduate studies took him to Ohio State University where he was instrumental in determining the structure of the antibiotic, streptomycin.

Two years on the staff of the University of Saskatchewan followed before he went to work at the Prairie Regional Laboratory of the National Research Council in 1949. Four years after this appointment Lemieux had successfully synthesized sucrose, common table sugar.

It was a feat that had been attempted unsuccessfully by the world's top chemists for over 100 years. In 1954 Lemieux became Chairman of Chemistry and Dean of Pure and Applied Science at the University of Ottawa. Under his guidance it became an outstanding research centre. In 1961 Dr. Lemieux was appointed Professor of Organic Chemistry at the University of Alberta. Six years later he was named a Fellow of the Royal Society of London. Lemieux was the first western Canadian to receive the honour. It is the highest scientific distinction in the British Commonwealth. Past members of the Royal Society of London include the most outstanding scientists in recent centuries, such as: gravitation theorist Isaac Newton; inventor of the dynamo, Michael Faraday; evolutionist Charles Darwin and medical innovator Joseph Lister.

Lemieux was chairman of the division of organic chemistry from 1966 to 1973. Scientific research, he felt, should solve real problems and have real payoffs. Lemieux had long advocated more high-technology Canadian-owned industries. He started Raylo Chemicals in 1967. He is also founder, president and research director of R & L Molecular Research Ltd. and president of Chembiomed Ltd.

One of the main thrusts of Chembiomed's work is a new approach to typing human blood. A synthetic antigen was produced and used in the manufacture of a better blood typing serum. The substance has helped answer questions about differences in human blood types.

Lemieux's works in the development and application of scientific knowledge continue to make major contributions to science and Canadian business.

William Herbert Swift

One of Alberta's foremost leaders in education began his career as a provincial administrator attending to 12 log schools.

William Herbert Swift graduated with a B.A. from the University of Alberta in 1924 and received his teacher training in 1925 at the Calgary Normal School. After teaching for two years he returned to university and received Master of Arts (1928) and Master of Education (1930) degrees. His Ph.D was obtained from Stanford in 1941.

Swift first served a term as Residence Dean at the Olds School of Agriculture. It was followed by five years as Inspector of Schools in the Athabasca region from 1930 to 1935. Dr. Swift says of this time, "Five years in the largely wilderness inspectorate of Athabasca during the depression provided an endless series of challenges, physical and organizational... The territory was immense, from the west end of Lesser Slave Lake to thirty-five miles southeast of Lac La Biche, and from Clyde in the south to Fort McMurray in the north. There was no gravel road whatsoever in the territory, only crude dirt roads." Dr. Swift was instrumental in creating twelve new school districts out of this territory, with a log schoolhouse in each one. Swift also speaks warmly of his rural and normal school teaching days; but his posts became more and more responsible in the field of education. After a succession of appointments Dr. Swift became the Deputy Minister of Education for the province of Alberta in 1946.

Swift was soon active in completing the establishment of school divisions and the later development of counties. He administered the

124

systematic extension of equalized financial support for school authorities, culminating in the School Foundation Program.

During his 20 years as a deputy minister he transferred teacher training to the University of Alberta, established a system of student aid, extended vocational education and worked for the creation of the School for the Deaf. In 1966 Swift left to take over chairmanship of the newly-established Universities Commission.

Dr. Swift's accomplishments in a long career as an educator became too numerous to mention. Among his honours was the Meritorious Alumni Golden Jubilee Award conferred by the University of Alberta in 1961. Dr. Swift has also received honorary doctorates from the universities of Alberta, Calgary and Lethbridge.

He earned, as well, the continuing affection and respect of fellow administrators and educational colleagues throughout North America.

Eric L. Harvie

He was born a dentist's son in Orillia, Ontario. At the peak of his career he was rumoured to be the richest man in Canada. He died as a person who – in the words of *Time Magazine* – "gave everything back and then some."

Eric Lafferty Harvie came to Calgary with his parents in 1911 when he was 19. He studied law at Osgoode Hall in Toronto and the University of Alberta. In 1915 he joined the Calgary law firm of his uncle, J.D. Lafferty, a former mayor of that city. Then the First World War intervened. While fighting as an infantryman in 1916 he was seriously wounded at the Somme. He later joined the Royal Flying Corps.

Back in Canada he married

Dorothy Jean Southam, who came from a wealthy publishing family whose holdings included the Calgary *Herald*. Yet Eric Harvie didn't need his in-laws to provide him with financial security. In the 1920s and 30s, along with many other Calgarians, he began to dabble in land purchases around the oil fields of Turner Valley.

Dabbling turned serious in 1944 when he bought mineral rights to almost half a million acres of land around Leduc, just south of Edmonton. Stories of what he paid for that land ranged from $4,850 to $110,000. The exact figure is not important, because on February 13, 1947 an oil well called Imperial Leduc #1 blew in and began the petroleum boom in Alberta.

The Leduc find was quickly followed by a major oil discovery at Redwater — also on land controlled by Eric Harvie. Within five years he had amassed a fortune reported to exceed $100,000,000.

Harvie wasn't content to sit back and watch his money grow. He began to collect things: paintings, Indian rattles, treaties and other artifacts. British medals, arms and armour. He had a vision of preserving the mixed cultural heritage of western Canada. Treasures bought around the world were stored in Calgary factory buildings.

In 1966 his vision matured when he presented his collection of over 200,000 items to the Alberta government, along with an endowment of $5 million.

Ten years later the Glenbow-Alberta Institute was opened in downtown Calgary — a $12 million monument chronicling the development of the prairies and Alberta in particular. It was by no means the only tangible evidence of Eric Harvie's generosity. The Devonian Foundation he had established in 1956 financed a 2½-acre covered park in Calgary called the Devonian Gardens. It also gave money to numerous Alberta towns to spruce up their main streets.

Harvie's philanthropy was wide and varied. The Calgary Zoo, Heritage Park, the Calgary Allied Arts Centre, the Fathers of Confederation Centre in Charlottetown, P.E.I., the Banff School of Fine Arts — all benefitted from his gifts. The Scottish town of Bannockburn received a mounted statue of King Robert the Bruce, and Calgary was given a duplicate.

The Crowfoot Indians called him *Natos-api* — "Old Sun." Yet Eric Harvie preferred to remain in the shadows, in spite of his conspicuous charity. He had collected everything from Mason jars to Queen Victoria's wardrobe: bloomers and all! When his collection found a permanent home at the Glenbow, however, it was more than a year after Harvie's death.

His contribution to western Canada seemed understated in 1957 when he was presented with an honorary degree from the University of Alberta: "Mr. Harvie is one of those men who has been endowed with a sense of history and he has the energy and ability to do something about it."

W.O. Mitchell

Alberta's most popular writer isn't an Alberta writer at all. He lives in Alberta, but W.O. Mitchell was born and raised in Saskatchewan. His best-loved novel was set in that province. Perhaps it is most accurate to describe W.O. Mitchell as an all-Canadian storyteller. But he's also a teacher and performer who has worked as a salesman, lifeguard, seaman, editor and high school principal.

William Ormond Mitchell was born in Weyburn, Saskatchewan, in 1914. His experiences in that farm community during the Depression provided much of the material for his later writing. Because of a medical problem young Billy Mitchell was taken to Florida by his family for part of his secondary education. Later he studied at the universities of Manitoba and Alberta.

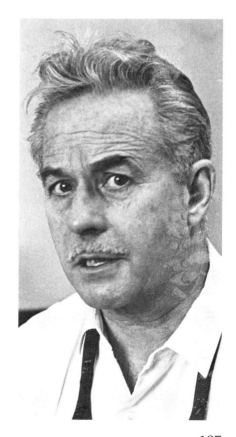

His first novel, *Who Has Seen the Wind?*, was published in 1947. It tells the story of a young boy coming to grips with the cycle of life and death. The book has been a favourite of two generations of Canadian readers. It has sold over 50,000 copies a year and formed the basis of a successful motion picture.

During the 1950s W.O. Mitchell's radio series, *Jake and the Kid*, was regular entertainment in Canadian homes from coast to coast. Several of the scripts were assembled into a book which won the Leacock Award for humour in 1961.

He has published other novels – *The Kite* in 1962 and *The Vanishing Point* in 1973. He has also received other tributes, including honorary degrees from Canadian universities and the Chalmers Award in 1976 for his play, *Back to Beulah*.

Another Mitchell play, *The Black Bonspiel of Wullie MacCrimmon*, has appeared in various forms and has been a hit with theatre audiences across Canada. It is the story of a man who makes a deal with the Devil to win the country's biggest curling competition.

Mitchell describes writing as "just like lying." But, he adds, "when you can suspend disbelief, then it's a magic lie." W.O. Mitchell beguiles his readers into suspending their disbelief. He does it with a mixture of wry humour, accurate dialogue and distinctive twists of plot and pacing.

He has influenced other writers in his roles as writer-in-residence and teacher of creative writing at various Canadian universities. He also influenced them as fiction editor for *Maclean's* magazine from 1948 to 1951.

During his years with *Maclean's* W.O. Mitchell discovered the Alberta town of High River. He soon moved his family there and they stayed for several years. Later they moved to Calgary where he continued to teach, write and grow orchids.

His readers know him for his books, plays and short stories. Thousands of others know him as a platform performer who tells his own yarns in a voice of dust and honey.

Author Rudy Wiebe perhaps describes him best: "Canada's most marvelous word-spinner."

Walter MacKenzie

Edmonton's stature as a centre for medical research is largely due to the efforts of Dr. Walter Campbell MacKenzie. For 15 years Dr. MacKenzie was Dean of the University of Alberta's Faculty of Medicine. His contribution to its development was such that the university's $140-million health science building will bear his name.

A distinguished surgeon, Dr. MacKenzie dedicated much of his life to training other surgeons. "I'm always interested in doing anything that will improve medical service...in particular, teaching," he has said.

For him, research was at the core of a doctor's requirements, along with a will to work hard.

Walter Campbell MacKenzie was a hotel proprietor's son from Glace Bay, Nova Scotia. He trained at Dalhousie, McGill and the University of Minnesota before interning in surgery for four years at the famous Mayo Clinic in Rochester, Minn. In 1938 he set up private practice in Edmonton. World War II intervened and MacKenzie served six years as surgical consultant with the Royal Canadian Navy. Then he returned to Edmonton where he would spend nine years as a professor and Chairman in the U. of A. Surgery Department before becoming Dean of Medicine in 1959.

His successor, Dr. D.F. Cameron, summed up Dr. MacKenzie's international reputation with the words, "From Peking to Moscow to the Arctic to the jungles of Africa, mention Edmonton and they will say, 'I have a good friend there in Walter MacKenzie.'"

Certainly MacKenzie's work brought him international recognition. He held membership in 25 medical societies and was president of half of them. He headed both the Royal College of Physicians and Surgeons of Canada and the American College of Surgeons.

Numerous honours came his way. For two years he was Honorary Surgeon to Her Majesty Queen Elizabeth. The Canadian Medical Association gave him its F.N.G. Starr award, which is known as the "Victoria Cross of Canadian Medicine." This put him in the company of such noted Canadian doctors as Banting, Best and Penfield. Non-medical honours included a Centennial Medal and the Order of Canada.

When he retired from the U. of A. in 1974 his name was mentioned as a possible successor to Lieutenant-Governor Grant MacEwan. He did not receive that position, but remained active as executive director of the provincial Cancer Hospitals Board.

Dr. MacKenzie was also chairman of a provincial task force on highway deaths and suicide. That group made 78 specific recommendations to reduce traffic injuries. Many were controversial, including reduced speed limits and compulsory use of seat belts.

Before his death in 1978 Dr. MacKenzie became an outspoken critic of the effect of medicare on doctors' morale.

Walter Campbell MacKenzie was a distinguished teacher and administrator. Before everything else, though, he was a doctor. Even with his university duties he set aside two mornings each week to perform surgery and two afternoons for consultation.

As always, at the core of this man of medicine was his devotion to research. It will continue under his name in Alberta in a world-class health sciences building.

James Gladstone

Few could imagine that one of the young Blood Indians using beef ribs to skate on the iced-over Belly River would someday become the first native to be appointed to the Canadian Senate. Certainly not James Gladstone, known as "Many Guns" or *Akay-na-muka* in Blackfoot. But the courage that James showed in his early years might have indicated that great things could be in store for him.

Born in Mountain Hill, Alberta, in 1887, James was sent to St. Paul's Anglican Mission School when he was seven. That first year he was tormented by a group of older boys who liked to make him the butt of their jokes. Their favourite trick was to hurl

James into the Indian graveyard when the supervisor wasn't looking. The Blood Indians didn't bury their dead but wrapped them in blankets and placed them in the trees. At first James was terrified but, when no ghosts appeared, he got brave enough to poke through the burial bundles. Here he found two skulls that he managed to sneak into the dormitory and hang above the beds of his tormentors. The two boys fainted and several others screamed when the ghoulish relics were found.

No one ever discovered who did it. But one of the ringleaders must have suspected for shortly afterwards he became James' good friend and the jokes stopped.

While still a schoolboy he helped the Royal North-West Mounted Police catch an escaped murderer. James led them to the tell-tale footprints the convict had left in the snow.

At 18, perhaps in recognition of his help to them years before, the RNWMP hired him as chief scout and interpreter for their base at Fort MacLeod. That same year he met and married Janie Healy, the daughter of a prominent Blood Chief. Her Blackfoot name was *Pok-otun*, or "Little Daughter."

After their marriage James served as a mail carrier for the Blood Indian Agency. When the First World War broke out in 1914 he put large areas of the Blood Reserve into crop to help the war effort. His efforts at grain farming and cattle raising proved so successful that many Bloods followed his example and became farmers and ranchers themselves.

Janie and James had six children over the course of these uncertain years. But, thanks to James' willingness to try new methods of farming, the children never went hungry. He was first on the reserve to buy a tractor. He also began the use of power machinery and chemical fertilizers, and was the first to have electricity in his home.

Word of Gladstone's hard work and success eventually spread throughout the province. He was voted president of the Indian Association of Alberta, a position he held for nine years.

The following year James Gladstone was appointed to the Senate of Canada, the first native senator in Canada's history.

He served prominently on a joint Senate-Commons committee on Indian Affairs. Suggestions of this committee led to treaty Indians becoming eligible to vote in federal elections in 1962.

True to his Indian name, Many Guns fought and won many battles before dying of a heart attack in 1971. Gladstone Mountain in southern Alberta is a tribute to a man who served as an example to all Canadians.

Maxwell Bates

"I am an artist, who, for forty years
Has stood at the lake edge
Throwing stones in the lake.
Sometimes, very faintly,
I hear a splash."
Maxwell Bates certainly heard a splash in 1928. The stone he had
thrown into the lake was an abstract painting called *Male and Female
Forms.* It was the first of its kind exhibited in Calgary. Public reaction
was so hostile that Bates was expelled from the Calgary Art Club. A
similar fate befell his colleague, W.L. "Roy" Stevenson.

Painter and art commentator
Ron Bloore has called Bates
and Stevenson "the most advanced painters in western
Canada during this period."
Maxwell Bates was born in
Calgary. He worked for his
father's architectural firm in
1924 before enrolling in the
Provincial Institute of Tech-
nology and Art (now the Alberta College of Art). As a
painter he pioneered in the
style of painting known as
abstract expressionism.

In 1931 he went to England
on a cattle boat to study paint-
ing and architecture. For most of the next decade his name was
associated with a school of artists known as the Twenties Group. His
income from art was augmented by jobs selling water softeners and
vacuum cleaners.

Max Bates enlisted in the British Army in 1939. He spent most of
World War II as a prisoner of war working in German salt mines. In
prison camp he ran art classes and got involved in camp theatrics,
including acting in a production of *Twelfth Night.*

He returned to Calgary in 1946 to pursue both painting and
architecture. A few years later he went to New York to study at the
Brooklyn Museum Art School, but came back to Calgary in 1950.

His most striking creation as an architect is St. Mary's Cathedral in
Calgary which he designed with A.W. Hodges. It is a tall, neo-Gothic

building which dominates one of the city's main streets.

Bates was a master of many styles. He and another artist, John Snow, pioneered in lithographic techniques in western Canada. Bates' own work in oils and watercolour often threw out normal space relationships to emphasize the psychological relationships of his subjects.

Many of his paintings are considered bizarre, grotesque, gloomy or satiric, and he has been compared with a number of major artists including Picasso and Max Beckman (with whom he studied in Brooklyn). Yet the noted critic Robin Skelton called him "one of the most powerful, original and profound painters of his generation."

Maxwell Bates often turned to writing – particularly poetry – to express the currents of his thought. He advocated an openness, a *naiveté* through which the artist could communicate the essential character of his subjects. "The naive painter," he wrote, "is a Humanist making plastic comments on the residue of daily life."

Bates suffered a stroke in 1961 which paralyzed the left side of his body. He was forced to give up architecture, but retired to Victoria and continued to paint until his death in 1980.

Frank McMahon

Many fortunes have been made in Alberta through a combination of shrewd analysis, hard work and good luck. It was true for Frank McMahon, and the "luck of the Irish" came through more than once.

Francis Murray Patrick McMahon was born in Moyie, British Columbia. After three years of university he worked as a diamond driller. Then he came to Turner Valley in southern Alberta. With his brothers, George and John, he started drilling for oil under the company name of West Turner Petroleums.

From 1935 to 1939 the luck wasn't with them. Finally they struck it rich with a well yielding 32,000 barrels of oil a day. A holding company, Pacific Petroleums, emerged. In 1947 MacMahon bought into the huge Leduc oil field and the next year his luck really turned bad – or so it seemed.

McMahon's Atlantic #3 well "came in" with such force that it was immediately out of control. For six months it spewed oil onto the countryside: one and a half million barrels, together with trillions of cubic feet of gas.

The ground softened and the drilling rig collapsed, snapping electrical cables and setting off a shower of sparks. The mammoth lake of oil caught fire. For 56 hours it raged, the most spectacular well fire in Canadian history. Finally the well was plugged with a combination of coiled cable, golf balls and chicken feathers.

Enter that fabled Irish luck. The publicity brought the vast reserves of Leduc to world attention. "Pacific Pete" was flooded with offers of investment money. Frank McMahon made a million dollars in six months. He borrowed four times that much from U.S. sources and embarked on a wildcat search for oil and gas in the Peace River area of British Columbia. The energy was there, sure enough, but Mc – Mahon needed a way to move the gas to markets in Washington and southwestern B.C. The result was Westcoast Transmission Ltd. which he created in 1949. He had persuaded the Social Credit government of B.C. to permit private gas drilling on Crown reserves in 1947 and had bought up the first three drilling permits. Now, after clearing up legal obstacles on both sides of the Canada-U.S. border, Westcoast was able to build a 700-mile gas pipeline 30 inches in diameter. McMahon has been given credit for the development of British Columbia's oil and gas industry.

That McMahon luck, backed by analysis and work, clicked in other areas as well. His investments in Broadway musicals paid off with such blockbusters as "Pajama Game" and "Damn Yankees." One of his many racehorses, Majestic Prince, won both the Kentucky Derby and the Preakness, two of the jewels in thoroughbred racing's Triple Crown.

Luck was with him as well when he established Alberta Distillers in the 1950s. While the company's first batch of whisky was aging he convinced his managers that the distillery should also make vodka,

134

which requires no aging. Perhaps he knew somehow that one year later a vodka-drinking craze would hit New York and the market would be assured. Or was it just luck?

Frank McMahon's business successes allowed him to maintain residences in several cities. He chose Vancouver as his retirement home. Yet his name is most noticeable in Calgary.

Not Frank McMahon the oilman, of course. Not even the race-horse owner or Broadway "angel." But Frank McMahon the backer of the local football team, the Calgary Stampeders. The team's home – compliments of brothers George and Frank – is a Calgary landmark, the McMahon Stadium.

1961 - 1970

A Changing Harvest

Resource development continues to transform the economic structure of Alberta. New rail lines push north; the tar sands are tapped; and an industrial base begins to develop in what was once a farm province.

Al Oeming

Albert Frederick Oeming was born in Edmonton but found himself curiously at home in the South Pacific by his late teens. As a graduate from Strathcona High School during World War II he immediately joined the armed services. Al served in the Pacific with the Royal Canadian Navy Voluntary Reserve. It gave him the opportunity to study the exotic wildlife of Australia, New Zealand and the South Sea Islands. The experience ignited a spark in the young man from Alberta. He returned to take a B. Sc. in Zoology from the University of Alberta in 1955.

He was now 30 and his well-developed love of nature and wildlife had shaped him into an ardent conservationist. That same year he helped persuade the government to ban the killing of grizzly bears in the Swan Hills region. As a protected zone, it could now be used as a source of valuable information about the vanishing species and perhaps preserve this important animal from extinction.

Oeming was more than just an advocate of conservation. He had a specific dream. In 1957 he bought 500 acres of land southeast of Edmonton and began to build the Alberta Game Farm. The idea was to build up a comprehensive collection of Canadian animals, especially Canadian hoofed animals, and to acclimatize exotic species that had never before been kept in such winter conditions. The farm was opened to the public on August 1, 1959. From modest beginnings it grew to one of the finest ungulate collections in the world.

Oeming, as director of the Game Farm, carries on active trading for exotic animals with nations all around the world. He continues to play a major role in pioneering new methods of keeping wild animals successfully in captivity.

In 1956 Al was elected a Fellow of the London Zoological Society and, in 1969, was awarded the Everly Medal (U.S.A.) for excellence in conservation. He was president of the Edmonton Zoological Society for nine years. In 1972 he received an honorary doctorate of Laws from the University of Alberta.

He has created wide public exposure to ideas and experiences of conservation. He speaks publicly on conservation, narrating wildlife films and, in 1971, was featured in an hour-long National Geographic Society TV special, "Journey to the High Arctic."

His work continues to bring world-wide attention to conservation in Alberta.

Violet Archer

In 1962 the Music department at the University of Alberta had just four faculty members. The newest was a petite Montreal woman with a giant reputation as a pianist, teacher and composer.

Violet Archer was born in 1913 to Italian-Canadian parents named Balestreri. At ten she began to take piano lessons. By the time she was 17 she was convinced that music would be her profession. In order to learn composition she studied all the orchestral instruments and began to write works for orchestra. "Everything I did pointed toward orchestral writing," she says. "I was mesmerized by the orchestra."

She enrolled in a music program at McGill University where she received a Bachelor of Music degree in 1936. Twelve years later she was granted a Masters degree from Yale University. In the meantime she had studied under the Hungarian composer Bela Bartok and the American Paul Hindemith. She also made her Montreal debut as a composer-pianist in 1942.

She did not restrict her composition to orchestral work. She has

written choral and chamber pieces as well as songs and a comic opera, *Sganarelle*. It was based on a play by Molière and had its debut in 1974 at the U. of A. Three years earlier she received her doctorate in Music from McGill.

One critic found in her music "...a loftiness of purpose, an economy of means and a mastery of musical media. Violet Archer," he wrote, "has a touch of genius."

Dr. Archer has written for a variety of instrumental combinations, but says her first love is writing for solo voice and piano. She describes herself as a "neo-classicist" but her name is often associated with the most contemporary of Canadian composers. In fact, she gave Alberta's first demonstration of electronic music in 1964.

Of more than 200 compositions her own favourite is a cantata called *The Bell*, based on John Donne's *Meditation XVII*. When another work of hers called *Psalmody* received its premiere performance in 1979 one critic called the occasion "Dr. Archer's finest hour."

Before coming to Edmonton as an associate professor she had been composer-in-residence at North Texas State University and the

University of Oklahoma. She has described the teacher's responsibility to students in these terms: "You must be interested in them, help them to unfold."

Violet Archer also feels the school system has an obligation to Canadian composers. "It's imperative for our schools to lead the way in performance of Canadian music and awareness of it."

The many honours Violet Archer has received include the Queen's Silver Jubilee Medal and a Canada Council senior fellowship in 1958 which allowed fulltime composing.

As a teacher of musical theory and composition she had emphatic opinions. She dismissed one work by Beethoven as "absolute nonsense" and described compositions by Richard Strauss as "dreadful stuff" and "boring."

As a composer she recognized the need for background and discipline. "If you are going to break the rules," she says, "you have to know them first."

Max Bell

Like many contemporary Canadians, George Maxwell Bell had grandparents who were prairie pioneers. His grandfather began his career as a blacksmith in the early 1880s and ended it as the Minister of Telephones in the second legislature in Saskatchewan. Max's father was a postal clerk who eventually became a western newspaper magnate.

141

In keeping with the family tradition, Max was to become a pioneer in his own right.

Born in Regina in 1912, he graduated from McGill University in Montreal to find Canada's business and industry crippled by the Great Depression. Unable to find work, the commerce graduate went prospecting for gold in the Kootenays. Three hard years of work were reduced to six ounces of gold which were stolen from him. Max would have returned home empty-handed had he not made money during this time by supplying the C.P.R. with railway ties.

He invested these profits in the Turner Valley oil field – one of the first significant oil finds in Alberta. It proved a very good choice for the one-percent shareholder.

Things took a turn for the worse when his father died in 1936. Max went to Calgary to clear up the estate and discovered that his father's newspaper, *The Albertan*, was in debt to the Royal Bank for half a million dollars. To bail out the paper Max borrowed $35,000 from four friends. Three years later all debts were paid.

His taste of success in the Turner Valley venture led him to further investments in the petroleum industry. He formed a company to buy rights on Crown oil reserves. When he did strike oil he formed a production company to refine and market it.

Reflecting on the exciting days of the petroleum boom, Bell said that some of his theories then were "hare-brained schemes." But they paid off.

The profits from the oil game allowed him to buy the *Edmonton Bulletin* in 1948. It folded three years later. He then bought controlling shares in three other newspapers. Soon he went into partnership with Victor Sifton, owner of several Canadian dailies. Their company, F.P. Publications Ltd., was soon to have daily newspapers in Calgary, Lethbridge, Winnipeg, Ottawa, Toronto, Vancouver and Victoria.

The holdings of this company made Max a recognized financial wizard. Now he had time to indulge in his hobbies. He was an avid fan of horse racing, so he bought a ranch and one hundred racing thoroughbreds. He collected Canadian art, played hockey and was an active and generous member of the Presbyterian Church.

When asked once how he accounted for his success, Max said, "The Lord put me in the right place at the right time with the right friends. I'm happy to say that we all made some money."

Max Bell died in 1972 at the age of 59. He left over $20 million to charitable organizations and bequeathed over $2 million to his family. People who knew this quietly successful man described him as "a reluctant inspiration to all."

Andy Russell

Andy Russell – outfitter, guide, writer and conservationist – was born on a ranch in southern Alberta. He dropped out of school after grade 10 in the 'Dirty Thirties' to earn a living trapping and busting broncos. By the age of 19 he had become a first class professional mountain guide, the youngest to hold a Grade A rating in the province.

Andy married Anne Riggall, daughter of the noted guide, Bert Riggall. Their honeymoon was a sheep hunt in the mountains.

In 1945 Andy began a writing career with a story in *Outdoor Life*. He took over Riggall's outfit in 1946, renaming it Skyline Pack Train. By the 1960s it became apparent that the pack train business was being killed by industrial encroachment. Andy took to cattle ranching.

In 1959 Andy helped organize the first successful expedition to capture Dall Sheep in the Yukon. From the film footage of this trip grew the plan for the Grizzly Country project. The idea was that Andy and his sons would study and film the life of the grizzly bear across 25,000 miles of the most rugged country on the continent.

Grizzly Country, the film and the book, represent a significant contribution to the world's understanding of grizzlies.

In an eventful life, Andy has been a big game hunter, an outfitter, a guide, trapper, rancher, a photographer, filmmaker, storyteller, expert marksman, a lecturer and a writer. He has outfitted and led many successful expeditions, including several to the Arctic.

Andy Russell's accomplishments and adventures could fill volumes of the best reading to be found. Despite limited formal schooling, his knowledge surpasses simple academic qualification.

143

Russell's honours include the Order of Canada (1977), Canadian Outdoorsman of the Year (1979) and the Jerry Potts Award, also in 1979. He is a member of the Explorers Club of New York, an honour which he holds in common with Lowell Thomas, John Glenn and Jacques Cousteau.

Andy Russell has now written six books and continues to be a voice for the wilderness.

John Decore

John N. Decore – teacher, lawyer, politician and judge – was not one to tolerate intolerance. When he retired as Chief Judge of the District Court of Alberta in 1979 a colleague said, "Some members of minority groups are tempted sometimes anxiously to seek acceptance; John Decore demanded it as a right." He had Ukrainian ancestry and was proud of it.

He was born in 1909 and took his early schooling in Andrew and Vegreville. During the Depression he taught school to finance the study of law at the University of Alberta. He received his law degree in 1938 and began to practise in Vegreville. Before long his firm had branches in St. Paul and Edmonton.

As a Liberal, John Decore was elected in 1949 to represent Vegreville in the House of Commons. He was re-elected

in 1953 but did not run in the 1957 election which brought the Progressive Conservatives into office.

In the House John Decore often advocated the rights of immigrants and minority groups. From *Hansard*, June 13, 1950:

"Too often in the past have we found people pre-judiced because of a man's colour, or because of the church he attends, or because of his racial origin, or because his name does not sound Anglo-Saxon."

While in Ottawa he was an advisor to the Secretary of State for External Affairs, Lester B. Pearson. As a member of Canada's delegation to the United Nations he spoke on various humanitarian issues before the world organization. During that period his chief, Lester Pearson, received the Nobel Peace Prize. In 1957 John Decore nominated "Mike" Pearson as national leader of the Liberal Party.

In 1957 he also left politics to spend more time with his family. The Decores and their three sons (who would all follow their father into the legal profession) moved to Edmonton. John helped establish a chair of Ukrainian Studies at the University of Alberta. He also became the first president of the Ukrainian Professional and Businessmen's Club in 1960.

John Decore was named a Queen's Counsel in 1964. The same year he was appointed Chief Judge of the District Court of Northern Alberta. During 15 years on the Bench he was instrumental in amalgamating the northern and southern divisions of that court. This led, in 1979, to the merger of the district court with the Trial Division of the Alberta Supreme Court into a new judicial body, the Court of Queen's Bench.

The man known affectionately by his fellow judges as the "Iron Uke" received an honorary doctorate from the U. of A. in 1980. He advised the graduates not to become "...so self-satisfied that you fail to see that others are less advantaged nor...so self-important or God-like that you exempt yourselves from the certain obligations in our society."

In his many careers and in his personal life, John Decore had accepted those obligations.

Grant MacEwan

One of Grant MacEwan's biggest complaints about the world was conformity. "Everyone wants to conform, to be 'the same as the other fellow.'" Many might disagree but no one could ever accuse Grant MacEwan of being ordinary. As a farm boy, student, civil servant, agriculturist, author, lecturer, show-ring judge, politician and public servant he never allowed himself to follow the beaten path.

Grant's parents were pioneers, not once but twice. His mother and father were both from Nova Scotia and came to settle north of Brandon, Manitoba, to do mixed farming. Grant was born there in 1902.

But the MacEwan family's life was soon to change dramatically, and when his family asked six-year-old Grant what he thought of their plans to sell the farm and move to Brandon he said, "This is the most important day of my life." And he was right. Once in Brandon, Grant entered two worlds — the world of the successful student who played hockey and baseball and the world of business. By the time he was 12 years old he had discovered many ways of earning a dollar, from selling newspapers to running the local grocery store.

Seven years after the MacEwans moved to Brandon property values crashed and so did the family fortunes. It was time to become pioneers again and they moved west to Melfort, Sakatchewan. Grant was 13 and was expected to do a man's work, turning the family patch of bald prairie into a farm.

Six years later Grant had to make a choice — to go to agricultural college or to stay in Saskatchewan and farm on his own. He decided to go the academic route, which evolved into a 23-year-long career as professor and dean in agriculture at the universities of Saskatchewan and Manitoba. He was soon to earn an international reputation as an agricultural advisor and writer of western Canadian history.

During this period of his life he met and married a schoolteacher named Phyllis Cline. Early in their marriage he warned her that he didn't plan to spend his life gathering moss while waiting to collect a university professor's pension.

He was true to his word. In 1951 he got an unexpected opportunity to run as the Liberal candidate in a federal by-election in Brandon. He had doubts about accepting the nomination and asked the advice of a friend who had spent many years in politics.

"What would you do?" he asked the politician. The politician thought about it for a while and finally said, "Grant, I'd pray."

If his prayers were answered they were answered in an unexpected way. Grant was thoroughly beaten in the by-election. He was later glad he had lost. Winning would have meant leaving his beloved West for Ottawa.

His next opportunity to enter politics was at the civic level and he became an alderman in Calgary. His political career took off at that point. He went on to become leader of the Alberta Liberal party in 1959 and was sworn in as Lieutenant-Governor of Alberta in 1966. He held that position until 1974.

While in public office he continued writing books, working early in the morning and late at night on buses, trains and airplanes. Now officially "retired," he continues to work as a writer as well as teacher, conservationist and broadcaster.

Roland Michener

The third Governor-General of Canada born in this country was a native of Lacombe, Alberta. Daniel Roland Michener seemed destined for statecraft. His father led Alberta's Conservative party for ten years and later became a senator.

Just after "Roly" was born in 1900 the family moved to Red Deer. The future governor-general was remembered there as "a nice little boy with wavy hair."

In high school he owned a pair of cows. Their milk supplied the family and also provided money to help further his education. His studies at the University of Alberta were briefly interrupted in 1918 for service in the First World War. When he graduated in 1920, however, he received both the Governor-General's Medal for top student and a Rhodes Scholarship to study law in England.

At Oxford University he excelled in sports, especially track and hockey. One hockey teammate was Lester B. Pearson who later became Prime Minister of Canada. Although they supported different political parties, "Roly" and "Mike" became close friends. They were partners in the Canadian Open Tennis Tournament one year, but lost in the first round.

After Oxford, Roland Michener returned to Canada and set up a successful law practice in Toronto. By 1943 he had decided to enter politics. In 1945 he was elected to the Ontario legislature and served as Provincial Secretary until he lost his seat in 1948.

Five years later he became a member of parliament. With the Conservatives in power in 1957, he was elected Speaker of the House of Commons. He held that post until his defeat in the 1962 election.

Early in his career Roland Michener explained his political philosophy: "My special approach to politics is the legal rights of the people and constitutional safeguards and guarantees. I think there is a fundamental contribution to be made in guaranteeing these rights."

In 1963 he chaired a royal commission on local government in Manitoba. The next year his old friend Lester Pearson named him Canada's High Commissioner to India. The man he succeeded, Chester Ronning, was also an Albertan (see page 91).

In the Commons and abroad, Roland Michener had a reputation for dignity and fairness. He learned to speak both French and Hindi. And he was always impeccably dressed. In India he was one of the few diplomats to wear a suit and vest in even the hottest weather.

When Governor-General Georges Vanier died in 1967, Mr. Pearson again turned to his friend. Roland and Norah Michener presided at Rideau Hall until 1974. It was a period noted for warm and gracious hospitality.

Roland Michener was probably the most physically-fit governor-general in Canadian history. Even in his seventies, his wavy hair and trim moustache a snowy white, he could be seen jogging briskly on the Rideau Hall grounds. The lessons he learned from sports served him well as a politician and statesman: "a tolerant approach to everyone and a dislike of jealousy and interracial disputes."

148

Ernest Manning

He was a tough-minded administrator and a deft politician who ruled longer than any other provincial premier in Canadian history.

Ernest Charles Manning grew up as a farmboy in Rosetown, Saskatchewan. One Sunday morning he heard a radio broadcast that changed his life and the life of Alberta. The speaker was William

Aberhart, a Calgary school principal and fundamentalist preacher. Ernest Manning was spellbound. When Aberhart announced that he was establishing a school called the Prophetic Bible Institute, the young Manning packed his bags and became the first student to enroll. He lived in the Aberhart home and became an ardent disciple of "Bible Bill." Physically, the two men could not have been more dissimilar. Aberhart was a tall, rotund man, while Manning was short and slender. Philosophically, though, they were twins.

After graduation Ernest became a lecturer and right-hand man to the founder of the Prophetic Bible Institute. He shared Aberhart's conversion to the Social Credit money theory as the answer to the Great Depression. When Aberhart became premier in 1935 Ernest Manning became a cabinet minister – Canada's youngest at the age of 26.

William Aberhart died in 1943 and the Social Credit caucus unanimously chose Manning to succeed him. There were predictions that the end was near for Social Credit. The new leader knew differently. Manning led the party to victory after victory, often with overwhelming majorities. And he presided for 25 of the most dynamic years of Alberta's history, as the province moved from a quiet farm-based economy to a bustling centre of the energy industry.

He also took over the radio evangelism of Aberhart. His program, "Canada's National Back to the Bible Hour," boasted a half-million weekly listeners across Canada. He didn't mix his political philosophy into the religious message as Aberhart had blatantly done. Still, the weekly exposure undoubtedly helped secure his political base.

Religion, politics and farming formed the trinity of Ernest Manning's life. He owned a 312-acre dairy farm just outside Edmonton. From time to time there were hints of scandal within his government, but his personal integrity was never challenged. Neither was the sincerity of his religious beliefs. "Religion isn't something you keep on a shelf and only take down on a Sunday," he often said.

As a politician, Ernest Manning was a professional. He held several cabinet portfolios himself, including those of Provincial Treasurer and Attorney-General. He demanded high performance from his other ministers, but he listened to their opinions, saying, "You can't learn anything when you're talking."

Still, he could bite back hard when his government came under attack.

In 1968 Manning retired as premier. The year before he had written a book called *Political Realignment: a Challenge to Thoughtful Canadians.* It suggested a new grouping of "social conservative" forces was needed in Canadian politics. At the same time he admitted that he thought Social Credit was dead as a political force at the federal level.

Many members of his party felt betrayed. The feeling grew after he retired to start a consulting firm. He accepted positions on the boards of several companies, including a bank. Social Credit had based much of its early program on opposition to the Canadian chartered banks.

When Ernest Manning was named to the Senate of Canada in 1970 it was another first. He was the first Social Credit member to be appointed to the Red Chamber.

Mel Hurtig

He might have become a furrier. For three years after high school he *did* work in his family's fur store in Edmonton – "...one of the most boring things I have ever done in my life." Finally, when a 300-pound customer complained that a fur coat made her look heavy, Mel Hurtig decided to call it quits.

The immediate result of that decision was a bookstore, which he started in 1956 with $1,000. "I had so little money and so few books that I turned them face outwards to make the shelves look full," he says.

The long-term result is one of the liveliest book publishing companies in Canada, Hurtig Publishers Ltd. It began with $30,000 in borrowed money and published seven titles during Canada's Centennial year, 1967. One of those books won the Governor-General's Award for poetry and Mel Hurtig, publisher, became an important person in Canadian literary circles. Over the years, Hurtig has published scores of Canadian bestsellers – all without leaving his native Edmonton.

When he set up that first bookstore in 1956 he had no experience in bookselling. Still, he liked to read and paid attention to customers' requests. Eventually his retail business developed into a chain of three Edmonton stores. Literary critic Nathan Cohen described Hurtig's main store as "the best-classified and most up-to-date in Canada."

Hurtig sold his stores in 1972 because, in his words, "Instead of being a bookseller, I had become an accountant." He turned to publishing Canadian books fulltime.

Fulltime? Not quite. A great deal of Hurtig's time and energy goes to promoting Canadian unity and Canadian economic independence. In 1970 he helped found the Committee for an Independent Canada, which he later served as national chairman. The group is dedicated to fighting foreign ownership of Canada's economy.

As one of the CIC's principal spokesmen, Hurtig received about 15 speaking invitations each week and accepted about three each month. "No one has travelled farther to cry 'rape' louder," wrote a *Financial Post* journalist.

Hurtig does not disguise his fascination with politics. He was an early supporter of Pierre Trudeau, and ran unsuccessfully as a Liberal candidate in the 1972 federal election. The next year, however, he left the party because of differences over the foreign ownership issue. During the campaign, Prime Minister Trudeau had described Hurtig as "a thorn" in his side.

One wall of Mel Hurtig's office consists of books he has published. On another wall is a Canadian map sporting pins to show the places he has spoken. As well, there is a bulletin board covered with newspaper clippings about Mel Hurtig, publisher and spokesman for Canadian nationalism.

He is an intense, wiry man with national stature. Author John Robert Colombo describes both Hurtig's vitality and his determination when he says, "If Canada disappeared, Mel could reconstruct it."

1971 - 1980

...So Shall They Reap

A new confidence emerges in the social, cultural and economic life of Alberta. The province becomes a consistent challenger in arts, sports and politics as prosperity continues to fuel its rapid expansion. Abundance brings fresh responsibilities and problems.

Peter Lougheed

Whenever Albertans have rejected a government, they have done it decisively. Monday, August 30, 1971 was no exception. That morning Peter Lougheed set the barometer in his Calgary home to "Change" before going to vote. Change came quickly. By evening, Alberta voters had approved Daylight Saving time, and they had made Peter Lougheed, at 43, their new premier.

The "sudden" change toward Lougheed's Progressive Conservatives had been six years in the making. When he became leader in 1965 the party had no members in the Alberta legislature. Now it had 49. Social Credit, which had formed the government for 36 years, was reduced to 25 seats.

No one who had known Peter Lougheed for long was surprised that he could achieve such a feat. Even in high school he had a reputation as an organizer. He had started the first student council at his school.

Edgar Peter Lougheed was born in 1928 into one of Calgary's leading families. His grandfather, Sir James Lougheed, was Alberta's first senator. His maternal great-grandmother had been a Metis woman. Another branch of the Lougheed family, spelling its name differently, had established the giant Lockheed aircraft corporation in California.

154

Like many other prairie families, the Lougheeds had been hit hard by the Depression. As a corporate lawyer and senior executive of the Mannix Corporation, Peter did much to restore the family's position before turning his attentions to politics.

While he was studying law at the University of Alberta he had excelled at football. They called him the "swivel-hipped half." Later he played professionally with the Edmonton Eskimos for two seasons.

From U. of A. he went to Harvard for a Masters degree in Business Administration. A summer training job with Gulf Oil took him to Tulsa, Oklahoma. There he witnessed the effects caused by the end of an oil boom and he was determined to do what he could to prevent the same thing happening in Alberta.

After August 30, 1971, he had the opportunity to try. World prices for oil and gas began to soar and drilling activity increased in Alberta – along with revenues to the provincial government. This gave Peter Lougheed the political muscle to make some demands on the federal government. His minimum terms: a greater voice for Alberta in national energy policy and observer status at oil and gas trade negotiations.

"If Alberta poker chips are involved at the poker table," he said shortly after becoming premier, "we will be at that table."

Later his government established the Heritage Savings Trust Fund to set aside a portion of provincial oil and gas revenues for the future. It quickly became one of the largest investment funds in the world and has lent money to several other Canadian provinces.

The Progressive Conservatives were re-elected with overwhelming majorities in both 1975 and 1979. Before the 1979 election, Peter Lougheed suggested that it would be his last as party leader. Nevertheless, he headed into his tenth year as Alberta's tenth premier still firmly at the helm. He was waging his battle for provincial rights in resource matters with renewed vigour.

Timothy Byrne

Education in Alberta has grown from a small fry assortment of country schools to a sophisticated and specialized network. Timothy Byrne has been an eyewitness to much of that change.

He was born in Minnesota in 1907 but came to Alberta as an infant when his parents decided to homestead in the Wasketanau area. After graduating from Camrose Normal School in 1925 he moved steadily up through the educational system to its loftiest positions.

Tim Byrne spent his first four years as a teacher in Radway before earning a Bachelor of Arts degree in History at the University of Alberta. From 1932 to 1937 he taught high school in Mirror while he continued his own studies. His thesis on Ukrainian nationalist organizations in north-central Alberta earned him an M.A. He later received his Masters degree in Education (U. of A.) and a doctorate in Education (University of Colorado).

Byrne taught for five years in Calgary. Then, in 1942, he was appointed school superintendent in Foremost. Five years later he received a similar position in the larger school district of Taber.

School consolidation was the big issue of the day. Byrne favoured the move to larger, centralized schools because of the expanded opportunities they offered students. In Foremost, at least, the parents approved the move because it resulted in improved roads for school bus routes. Of course, the scale of educational expenditure was quite different from today's. Tim Byrne was once involved in building a four-room school in Conquerville, complete with outdoor plumbing. Its cost: $28,000.

In 1949 he became a high school inspector in Calgary. From 1957 to 1966 he was the province's chief superintendent of schools. Then, in 1966, his career as an educational administrator took a major leap. He was appointed Alberta's Deputy Minister of Education.

Byrne's abilities and personality had helped him overcome barriers which might have inhibited others. Although he was a Roman Catholic, for example, he rose through a school system which was largely Protestant. As a deputy minister, as well, his political views differed from those of the ruling Social Credit party of the time. "I regarded myself as being very much a small-'l' liberal," he says.

In 1971 Tim Byrne took on a new challenge. The former deputy minister of education was appointed as the first president of Athabasca University. Although the new government was suspicious of many of the Social Credit appointees on the university's board, it eventually gave approval for Athabasca to offer correspondence courses on a five-year trial basis.

The university is still in existence, and Tim Byrne is proud of its record. "We opened a route to knowledge for more people," he says.

Tim Byrne's reputation as an educational administrator went beyond Alberta. He was president of the Canadian Council for Research in Education for two years. He also represented Canada at various international conferences on education. When he retired from Athabasca in 1976 he spent four years as visiting professor at the U. of A. continuing a life devoted to education.

Max Ward

From northern bush pilot to czar of one of the world's largest charter airlines...that's the flight plan followed by Maxwell William Ward, son of a C.N.R. ticket agent from Edmonton.

Max Ward began flying with the Royal Canadian Air Force in 1940, and for much of World War II served as flight instructor at various Canadian air bases. When war ended, he started flying commercially into the Northwest Territories.

In 1946 he took $4,000 he had saved and borrowed to make a down-payment on a three-passenger de Havilland *Fox Moth*. He now headed his own company, Polaris Charter Ltd. But the Air Transport Board saw the little biplane as inadequate for a charter company and refused Polaris a licence. Max teamed up with another company, Yellowknife Airways Ltd. It soon went sour and he had lost both his plane and his money.

Discouraged and broke, he moved to Lethbridge and joined his father-in-law in the construction business. By 1953, however, Max Ward was back in the flying business with a 14-seat de Havilland *Otter* and a fully-licenced company called Wardair.

That company *did* take off. By 1956 Wardair had 13 employees and was in a position to buy a full-bellied Bristol freighter.

Instead of prospectors and medical teams, Max Ward was now able to fly livestock, construction equipment and even prefabricated buildings into a rapidly-developing North. In 1961 Wardair acquired a four-engine Douglas DC-6AB worth $1.5 million. It was ideal for flying cargo into the Arctic when lakes were frozen solid. In the summer months it would be useless for that purpose. So Max decided to convert his new freighter into a passenger carrier. During 1962 it made eight trips over the North Pole to England, Denmark and Norway. Those European trips took 19 hours, plus a one-hour refuelling stop in Greenland. But the charter-flight concept seemed premature for western Canada. Traffic was lighter than Max Ward expected and the company lost $370,000. "We learned what overseas charters were about," he says. "The hard way."

In spite of his second major setback, Ward kept trying. He still had several bush planes operating into the North. By 1965 the charter business was on a solid footing. By 1969 he added a Boeing 727 and two 707s to his fleet. The signal that he had really arrived, however, was his purchase of a $25 million Boeing 747 in 1973.

Max Ward now heads an international chartering giant with offices in several countries and an annual budget well over $100 million. He has received many honours, such as membership in the Order of Canada, the Canadian Aviation Hall of Fame and the Order of Icarus. He has won both the Billy Mitchell award and the McKee Trophy for his contributions to air transportation.

Still, he has never lost sight of his beginnings. As Wardair added new 747s to its fleet, they were nicknamed after outstanding pioneers of Canadian flying - men like "Punch" Dickins and "Wop" May. The names are fitting company for Max Ward — once and always a bush pilot.

Maria Campbell

A book published in Toronto in 1973 has seared the consciences of many Canadians. It is called *Halfbreed*, and it is the life story of an Edmonton woman, Maria Campbell.

In a prose style which is eloquently direct, the author tells of the joys and crushing sorrows of growing up a "halfbreed" in northwestern Canada. Without bitterness she tells of raising, then losing, her orphaned brothers and sisters in northern Saskatchewan; of marrying for convenience at the age of 15; of falling into a life of prostitution, alcoholism and drug addiction on the West Coast.

Part of the story of Maria Campbell is the tragic story of Canadians who are neither Indian nor White, but yet are both. The rest of Maria Campbell's story is that of a successful author, writer-in-residence at the University of Alberta, whose work has been published in several languages.

Maria Campbell was born in northern Saskatchewan in 1940. Her father was an illiterate trapper. Her mother died when Maria was still in grade-school, leaving her to bring up seven younger brothers and sisters. Fortunately, the convent-educated mother had left her daughter with a love of literature and art.

Then there was Maria's great-grandmother, Cheechum, a powerful woman who lived to 104 and died after being thrown from a runaway wagon. Cheechum was probably the strongest positive influence on Maria's life. She instilled in her great-granddaughter a pride in her mixed-culture heritage, an awareness of the mystic side of life and a commitment to honesty and integrity.

In 1963, after a painful battle with drugs and alcohol, Maria Campbell moved from Vancouver to Edmonton and became active in the human rights movement. She involved herself in the struggles of women prisoners, battered wives and native persons. And she decided to tell the "halfbreed" story.

As a writer she has gone on to produce numerous radio plays. Other books on native topics include *People of the Buffalo, Riel's People* and *Little Badger and the Fire Spirit*; all aimed at younger readers.

She has also produced two film scripts for the National Film Board — *The Red Dress* and *Delivery*.

In 1979 Maria Campbell was appointed writer-in-residence at the University of Alberta for one year. She described the position as "like welfare for writers. They give you a pen and paper, telephone and office. I'm even on the dental plan this year!"

Maria Campbell is herself a grandmother now. Still she remembers the lessons of fairmindedness and optimism passed down by her own great-grandmother, Cheechum.

These lessons came out in her autobiography in this hopeful assertion:

> "I believe that one day, very soon, people will set
> aside their differences and come together as one.
> Maybe not because we love one another, but
> because we need each other to survive."

Joseph H. Schoctor

The name "Citadel Theatre" and the name "Joe Schoctor" are frequently mentioned in the same breath. Without Schoctor, many feel, there would be no Citadel.

The Edmonton-born lawyer, fund-raiser and drama producer is the son of a peddler and scrap dealer who immigrated from Russia in 1913. Joe's career took another turn. At 12 he discovered drama and pursued his interest throughout high school. At the University of Alberta he continued this interest (and, incidentally, played football for the Golden Bears).

In the 1960s his dramatic talents took him to New York, where he produced five plays on and off Broadway. When a woman asked why he wasn't producing plays in Edmonton, he took her question seriously. The idea of the Citadel was born.

Schoctor became campaign manager for the $6.6 million theatre, built on the old market place where Joe's father once ran a stall. The Citadel, an immense glass and steel case, encloses a complex of theatres, cultural facilities and restaurants. Its design won scores of awards.

"Theatre adds a dimension to the lives of people," says Joe. "They grow with it, sharing the glory and defeat of the distilled lives that are portrayed on the stage. Theatre enlarges the spirit, just as sports creates heroes. People live more; that's what it's all about. That's why I do it."

Schoctor is a successful lawyer and a member of the Order of Canada. In 1948 he helped found the Edmonton Eskimos Football Club.

His real gift to Edmonton, though, was the Citadel Theatre. "It's part of my life," he said in a 1981 interview. "I owe the Citadel much more than it owes me."

John P. Gallagher

"As smooth in manner as a kitten's wrist." That's how a *Maclean's Magazine* writer described John Patrick Gallagher, founder and chairman of Dome Petroleum Ltd. And in Ottawa, they call tax concessions he persuaded the federal government to make the "Gallagher amendments."

Jack Gallagher is a slim, handsome geologist born in Winnipeg in 1916. He's considered one of the shrewdest men in the Canadian oil patch and a "lone wolf" who follows his own advice. It has often meant going against the conventional wisdom of the industry he works in.

After studying geology at the University of Manitoba, "Smiling Jack" Gallagher had a brilliant 13-year career with Standard Oil. It involved working in 12 foreign countries, mostly in the Middle East and Latin America. He would make his biggest mark, however, in the Beaufort Sea of Canada's high Arctic. Dome expects to find oil and gas reserves there almost equal to the current national consumption.

161

Gallagher discovered the challenge of the North when he was a student working summers for $2.50 a day with the Canadian Geological Survey. That was in the 1930s. He never lost sight of the dream to capture the oil and gas riches of that region.

In 1950 he was faced with the decision of moving toward  Standard's head office or striking out on his own. A group of American investors asked his help to buy into Canadian energy resources, and the decision was easy for Jack Gallagher. He became an independent explorer – a wildcatter. The company he started then has gone on to become one of the giants of the Canadian oil business. As the largest single shareholder, Gallagher is said to hold assets worth more than $25 million in Dome Petroleum alone. The company also holds a large slice of TransCanada Pipe Lines Ltd. It was purchased to strengthen Dome's position if a MacKenzie Valley pipeline is built to pipe Arctic oil to southern markets.

Jack Gallagher is not considered by his colleagues – or by himself – to be an outstanding geologist. He is respected for his ability to put together complicated business deals involving other people's money. An admiring competitor says, "He is really aggressive but has this wonderful ability to gore people and make them like it. He is capable of such empathy with an opponent, and of being so disarming, that the opponent doesn't realize that he is being beaten."

Says Gallagher: "Life is too short to not try to work things out between competing forces." Undoubtedly, this statement would be accompanied by a flash of the famous "Smiling Jack" smile from what one writer called "the most photogenic teeth in Canadian business."

While business is the cornerstone of the Calgary oilman's life, he

162

has other interests. He is a regular jogger. He was a member of the World Peace Foundation. And, although he didn't follow through on the idea, he once intended to leave the business world at the age of 50 to work for the United Nations.

The philosophy of "Smiling Jack" Gallagher is simple: "You only go through life once," he says. "And it's a lot more fun if you plough a different furrow, rather than the same furrow that everybody else has ploughed."

Ralph Steinhauer

The first Canadian Indian to serve as a provincial Lieutenant-Governor was born on Alberta's Morley Reserve in 1905.

Ralph Garvin Steinhauer's family name came from his great-grandfather who had been adopted by a childless couple named Steinhauer. The great-grandfather was the first Indian ordained as a Wesleyan minister. He built his mission at Whitefish Lake in northeastern Alberta.

Ralph's Indian name, *Omsokistikkeeweepow*, means "big farmer." True to the name, he now farms at Saddle Lake, 100 miles northeast of Edmonton.

Ralph spent 37 years as chief and councillor of the Saddle Lake reserve. In 1963 he became the first Indian ever to run for the Liberal party in a federal election.

Eleven years later he was appointed Alberta's tenth Lieutenant-Governor. He served in that capacity until 1979.

Steinhauer had always been active in Indian and agricultural organizations. He was founder, director and executive officer of the Alberta Federation of Indians and a board member of the Indian-Eskimo Association. He was president of the Alberta Indian Corporation, and worked with organizations for Indian and rural economic development. He has also been district president of the National Farmer's Union and was involved with Alberta Newstart and the Northern Development Council.

While Steinhauer was Lieutenant-Governor, he was the first Indian from another tribe to be made an honorary chief of the Blood Indian band in southern Alberta. The headdress of eagle feathers was placed on Mr. Steinhauer's head, and he received the title Chief Flying Eagle.

Ralph Steinhauer's accolades include a Medal of Service of the Order of Canada. He was made an officer of the Order in 1972.

Tommy Banks

Edmonton's 'Mr. Music' is an internationally-esteemed producer, pianist, composer, bandleader and arranger.

Tommy Banks may have received his broadest recognition for the CBC Television production The Tommy Banks Show, which ran for six years. But Tommy has been involved in almost every facet of Canadian music-making. *Maclean's Magazine* remarked that "it might be easier to list the things he doesn't do."

His professional career began in 1952 when he travelled with the Jammin' The Blues concert tour. At 17 he was musical director of the Orion Musical Theatre in Edmonton. When television came to Edmonton, Tommy became a TV performer for the CBC. In the mid-Sixties his show went national. After four more years, he switched to CITV and his work there paved the way for the successful Celebrity Concert Series. Banks has conducted orchestras in Montreal, Regina, Edmonton, Calgary and Hamilton. He is the most frequent guest conductor of the Edmonton Symphony and is widely acclaimed for his presentation of popular music by orchestras of such size.

Tommy has been part of more than six dozen internationally syndicated hour-long TV specials which have been seen in 55 countries. Banks also composed and arranged the score for the movie *Why Shoot the Teacher?*

As a conductor/pianist, he has worked with hundreds of stars in various media: Vikki Carr, Aretha Franklin, Paul Williams, Cleo Laine, Johnny Mathis, Doc Severinsen...the list goes on.

In 1978 Banks won a Juno Award and, that same year, the Grands Prix du Disque, Canada, for the best jazz release.

More honours for Tommy Banks, one of Canada's most accomplished musicians.

165

Don Smith

William Donald Smith was born with a knack for fostering talent in others. He took Alberta from a province with few top-calibre swimmers in the 60s to one of the strongest forces in the country.

The future member of the Alberta Sports Hall of Fame was born in 1921 in Port Colbourne, Ontario. He began teaching and coaching

aquatics 25 years later, and became one of the country's most inspirational swimming coaches and sports educators. In 1947 Don joined the University of Alberta physical education staff. He received his doctorate in Education from the University of Buffalo in 1957. Smith held many executive positions in swimming associations throughout his career. One of the most outstanding was as team manager to the National Swimming Championships involving the Canadian Olympic swimming and diving team at Mexico City in 1968. Another such outstanding responsibility was his work as chairman of the national swim team from 1967 to 1970. In 1970 he went to the Commonwealth Games in Edinburgh as assistant coach.

Smith acted as official representative of the Canadian Amateur Swimming Association to both the Canadian Olympic Association and the Canadian Pan American Games Association.

For seven years, Dr. Smith was a volunteer leader of the Boy Scouts and Wolf Cubs. He was the national president of the Canadian Association for Health, Physical Education and Recreation from 1967 to 1969.

The responsibilities Don Smith assumed in the world of sports go on and on. In recognition of his many achievements he was made a Fellow of the American College of Sports Medicine. He also received the Badge of Service and was given an honorary membership in the Canadian Red Cross Society. In 1974 he was inducted into the Alberta Sports Hall of Fame, along with his daughter, Becky.

His practice, as aquatic coach, was to get the masses swimming and then skim the cream off the top for international competition. His philosophy for the individual was "always finish what you start, and be ready to suffer hard times without pity."

Don saw a life's dream fulfilled in 1976 when two of his eight children, Becky and Graham, won medals at the Montreal Olympic Games.

Shortly after, on September 1, 1976, Don Smith died of cancer.

Joe
Clark

Canada's youngest prime minister was also the first born in the West. Charles Joseph Clark came from the foothills town of High River. He was sworn into office on June 4, 1979, the day before he turned 40.

A career in journalism, rather than politics, seemed likely for Joe Clark. Both his father and his grandfather had been editors of the High River *Times*. His own early ambition was to become a famous sportswriter. In fact, he did work briefly as a reporter during his college

167

days. But he had already been bitten by the political bug.

That happened when he was 17, on a scholarship visit to Ottawa. The Pipeline Debate in the House of Commons fascinated him, and the fascination deepened shortly after when John Diefenbaker came to High River. Joe Clark met him and decided that, like Diefenbaker, he would be prime minister some day.

As a boy, Joe was considered serious and shy, a "loner" more interested in books than in boyhood games. Later, while he was studying history at the University of Alberta, he began to blossom. He edited the student newspaper, *The Gateway*. He also became known as a prankster who once wheeled a shopping cart around the campus. In it was a bust of the German writer Goethe, adorned in sunglasses and a beret.

During this period he plunged seriously into politics. After graduation he served two terms as national president of the Progressive Conservative student federation. He also worked as private secretary to the Alberta party leader, W.J.C. Kirby.

Joe Clark had a flair for organization. After Peter Lougheed became leader of the Alberta Conservatives, Joe was hired as the party's provincial organizer. But a backroom role wasn't enough for him. In 1967 he ran as a provincial candidate in Calgary South, a seat which the Social Credit government considered one of its safest. He surprised everyone except himself by coming within 461 votes of winning.

He was soon back in Ottawa, working for one of the unsuccessful candidates for the party's national leadership. The man who won, Robert Stanfield, quickly hired him as his executive assistant.

In 1970, after polishing his French on a tour of Europe, Joe returned to Alberta to teach political science and complete his M.A. in that subject. Two years later he was elected as the member of parliament for Rocky Mountain in western Alberta. As an MP he demonstrated special interest in issues such as the environment, northern development, native rights and the concerns of youth.

When Robert Stanfield resigned in 1976, one of the surprising candidates for the leadership was Charles Joseph Clark. When the smoke had cleared after an exciting contest, the "Man from High River" was the new national leader of the Progressive Conservatives. Even then, so little was known about him that the press nicknamed him "Joe Who?"

By May 22, 1979, there was no doubt about who Joe Clark was. That day he was elected Prime Minister of Canada, breaking an 11-year reign by Pierre Elliott Trudeau. With the campaign help of his wife, Maureen McTeer, and his brother, Peter, he had also become the member of parliament from the new Alberta riding of Yellowhead.

Joe Clark had led the Conservatives back into office after 16 years in opposition. It wasn't to be a long stay. On December 13, 1979, the budget introduced by Finance Minister John Crosbie was defeated in a non-confidence vote and the Clark government fell. Two months later Pierre Trudeau was back as prime minister and Charles Joseph Clark was once more Leader of Her Majesty's Loyal Opposition.

The grassroots honesty of the first western-born prime minister had appealed to the Canadian voter. His philosophy? He stated it clearly when he was 27, to a student audience in Red Deer: "Look at your world with your own eyes, and do things that need to be done."

Index

ABERHART, William; Premier
of Alberta 72-74, 149, 150
Alberta: A Natural History 115
Alberta College of Art 96, 132
Alberta Distillers 134
Alberta Game Farm 138
Alberta and Great Waterways
Railway 18
Alberta Exhibition Assoc. 24
Alberta Flour Mills 24
*Alberta Golden Jubilee An-
thology* 115
Alberta Railway and Irrigation
Co. 28
Alberta School for the
Deaf 125
Alberta Society of Artists 93
Alberta Sun, The 26
Albertan, The 26, 142
Alix, Alta. 47
Allied Arts Council,
Calgary 94
Amateur Swimming Assoc.,
Canadian 166
Andrew, Alta. 144
ARCHER, Violet *139-140*
Art Foundation, Alberta 14
ATTRUX, Laura *117-119*
Aviation Hall of Fame,
Canadian 158
*Back to the Bible Hour,
Canada's National* 72, 150
Baker Street Irregulars 122
Banff, Alta. 39, 55, 45, 94
Banff School of Fine Arts
70, 88, 126
BANKS, Tommy *164-165*
BARNETT, John W. *71-72*
BARTLING, Hedwig *86-88*
Bassano, Alta. 39

BATES, Maxwell *132*
BEATTY, J.W. 95
Beaufort Sea 161
BELL, George Maxwell
141-142
BENNETT, Richard Bedford
64-66, 67, 76
Black Candle, The 37
Blood Indian Band 29, 130,
164
Bloodied Toga, The 115
Bragg Creek, Alta. 39
BREWSTER, Frederick Archi-
bald *45-47*
Brocket, Alta. 22
BROCKINGTON, Leonard
Walter *76-77*
BROOKE, Rupert 93
BROWN, Roy Capt. 59
BUGNET, Georges *77-79*
BUGNET, Therese 78
BULYEA, G.H.V. Lt.-Gov. 17
BURNS, Patrick *66-67*
BYRNE, Timothy *155-156*
Calgary Brewing and Malting
Co. 24, 34
Calgary Art Club 131
Calgary Gas Co. 34
Calgary Petroleum Products
Co. 34
Calgary Herald 126
Calgary Normal School 124
Calgary Public Library 93
Calgary Stampede 28, 29, 59,
67, 83
CALHOUN, Alexander *93-94*
CAMERON, Donald, Sen.
88-89, 129
CAMPBELL, Maria *159-160*
Camrose, Alta. 91, 93, 115

Camrose Normal School
  115, 155
Canadian Amateur Hockey
  Association   114
Canadian Author's Association
  115
Canadian Geological Survey
  162
Canadian Institute of Inter-
  national Affairs   94
Canadian Medical Association
  129
Canadian Western Natural Gas
  24
Carbon, Alta.   83
Cancer Hospitals Board   130
CARD, Charles Ora   28
Cardston, Alta.   22, 30
CARTER, Wilf   *83-85*
Celebrity Concert Series   165
China Mission   93
CHEECHUM   159-160
Chembiomed Ltd.   123
Citadel Theatre   160, 161
City of Edmonton   59
City of Libertines   114
Claresholm, Alta.   61, 74, 90
CLARK, Karl Adolph   *51-52*
CLARK, Charles Joseph; Prime
  Minister   *167-169*
CLARK, Peter   169
Clearwater (River)   39
Cochrane, Alta.   54
College of Art, Alberta   96
Committee for an Independent
  Canada   152
Commonwealth Games   166
C.P. Air   86
CLINE, Phyllis   146
COLLIP, James Bertram
  34-36
Conquerville, Alta.   155-156

CORBETT, E.A.   89
CROSS, Alfred Ernest   24-25
Crossfield, Alta.   54
Crow's Nest Pass, Alta.   67
"Cyclone"   29
"Dear Brutus"   70
DECORE, John N.   *144-145*
Delivery   160
Devonian Foundation   126
DICKINS, "Punch"   158
DIEFENBAKER, John; Prime
  Minister   53, 168
DINGMAN, Archibald Wayne
  32-34
Dome Petroleum Limited
  161, 162
DOUGLAS, Clifford H., Maj.
  69, 73, 74
Drama League, Alberta   70

Edmonton Bulletin   19, 142
Edmonton Commercial Grads
  Basketball Club   52-53
Edmonton Eskimos Football
  Club   155, 161
EDWARDS, (Bob) Robert
  Chambers   *25-27*
EDWARDS, Henrietta   37, 61
Eye Opener, Calgary   26

FAIRFIELD, William   *27-28*
Farmers' Equity Movement   44
Federation of Indians, Alberta
  164
Fire Spirit   160
Foremost, Alta.   156
Fort Chipewyan   22
Fort Edmonton   19
Fort MacLeod   29, 131
Fort McMurray   13, 22, 82
Fort Vermillion   59
GALLAGHER, J.P.   *161-163*

171

Gateway, The 168
Gay Dogs and Dark Horse 95
"Ginger Group" 69
GISSING, Roland 54-55
GLADSTONE, James, Sen.
 130-131
Explorers' Club 144
Glenbow-Alberta Institute 126
Golden Bears Football Club
 161
Grande Prairie 46
GOWAN, Elsie Park 70
Great Canadian Oil Sands
 (GCOS) 52
GREENFIELD, Herbert;
 Premier 48
GRIESBACH, William Antrobus
 40-41
Grey Nuns, the (Sisters of
 Charity) 20-22
Gulf Oil 155
Halfbreed 159
HALTON, Matthew 90-91
Hardisty, Alta. 115
HARDY, William George
 71, 114-115
HARVIE, Eric Lafferty 89,
 125-126
HARRIS, Lawren 95
HAYNES, Elizabeth Sterling
 69-71
Health, Physical Education and
 Recreation, Assoc. of,
Canadian 166
HEALY, Janie 131
HENRY, Billy 14
Heritage Park 126
Heritage Savings Trust Fund
 155
High Level, Alta. 119
High River, Alta. 14, 26, 128,
 167, 168

High River Times 168
Historical Society of Alberta
 18
HORNER, Vic 59
HODGES, A.W. 132
Hudson's Bay Co. 19, 21
HURTIG, Mel 151-152
Hurtig Publishers Ltd. 151
Imperial Leduc #1 126
Indian Corporation, Alberta
 164
INMAN, Don 14
I Remember 41
irrigation 27-28, 38-39
IRVINE, William 68-69
JACKSON, A.Y. 95
JACKSON, Frank 120
JACKSON, Mary Percy
 119-120
Jasper, Alta. 46
JOHNSON, Albert 60
Juno Awards 165
Keg River, Alta. 120
KERR, "Buck" Illingworth
 95-96
"Khaki College" 23
KIRBY, W.J.C. 168
Knights of the Round Table 93
Lac La Biche, Alta. 122
Lacombe, Alta. 47, 147
LACOMBE, Father Albert
 O.M.I. 13, 21, 67
Lac Ste. Anne, Alta. 21
La Forêt 78
Lake Louise, Alta. 57-58
LAURIER, Wilfrid; Prime
 Minister 17, 20
Leacock Award 128
Leduc, Alta. 26
LEE, Clifford E. 115-117
Lee, Clifford E., Foundation
 117

Legal, Alta. 78
LEMIEUX, Raymond Urgel
  122-123
Lethbridge, Alta. 27, 30, 87,
  157-158
Lethbridge Herald 91
Library Assoc., Alberta 94
LISMER, Arthur 95
Little Badger 160
London Zoological Society
  139
LOUGHEED, Edgar Peter;
  Premier of Alberta *154-155*,
  168
LOUGHEED, Sir James, Sen.
  64, 76, 154
MacADAM, Roberta 60
McCONACHIE, Grant *85-86*
McCLUNG, Nellie 37, *49-50*
MacDONALD, J.E.H. 95
McDOUGALL, George 13,
  14, 15
McDOUGALL, John 14
MacEWAN, Grant *146-147*
McGILLICUDDY, Daniel 26
McKINNEY, Louise Crummy
  37, *60-61*
MacLEAN, Margaret 86
MacKENZIE, Walter Campbell
  128-129
MACKENZIE KING, William
  Lyon; Prime Minister 23,
  65, 76
McMAHON, Francis Murray
  Patrick *133-134*
McTEER, Maureen 169
MANNING, Ernest Charles;
  Premier of Alberta 74,
  149-150
Markerville, Alta. 31
Mannix Corporation 155
MAY, "Wop" W.R. *58-60*,

158
MICHENER, Norah 148
MICHENER, Roland; Gover-
  nor-General *147-148*
Midnapore, Alta. 67
Mirror, Alta. 156
MITCHELL, William Ormond
  127-128
Morley Indian Reserve 164
Mountain Hill, Alta. 130
MURPHY, Emily Ferguson
  (Janey Canuck) *36-37*, 50
National Farmer's Union 164
National Film Board 160
National Geographic Society
  138
National Research Council
  122
Newstart, Alberta 164
Nipsya 78
NOBLE, Charles Sherwood
  74-75
NOLAN, Paddy 26
Non-Partisan League 61, 68,
  88
Northern Development
  Council 164
North Saskatchewan River 18
Northwest Territories 17, 20
  25, 38
Nutcracker, The 68
NuWest Homes 116
ODELL, Jean 121
OEMING, Albert Frederick
  138
Olds School of Agriculture
  124
OLIVER, Frank Bowsfield
  19, 41
Olympic Assoc., Canadian
  166
Olympic Games 166, 167

Orion Musical Theatre   165
Pacific Petroleums   133
Paddle Prairie, Alta.   119
PAGE, J. Percy   *52-53*
Pakan, Alta.   13
Pan American Games Assoc.,
  Canadian   166
PARLBY, Mary Irene   37,
  47-48
Peace River, Alta.   55, 92, 120
PEARCE, William   27, *38-39*
PEARKES, George R.; Lt.-
  Gov.   *82-83*
PEARSON, Lester B.   53,
  145, 147-148
People of the Buffalo   160
"Persons Case"   36-37, 50, 61
Pincher Creek, Alta.   90
Polaris Charter Limited   157
*Political Realignment, A Chal-
  lenge to Thoughtful
  Canadians*   150
Pipeline Debate   168
POTTS, Jerry   13
Prophetic Bible Institute   72,
  149
RADFORD, Tom   93
Radway, Alta.   155
Red Deer, Alta.   82, 147, 169
Red Deer (River)   39
Red Dress, The   160
Rich Valley, Alta.   78
Riel's People   159
RIGGALL, Anne   143
RIGGALL, Bert   143
Rocky Mountain House, Alta.
  55, 57, 168, 82
RONNING, Chester   *91-93*,
  147-148
ROPER, Elmer   116
Royal Canadian Navy Voluntary
  Reserve   138

Royal North-West Mounted
  Police   131
Royalite Oil   24
Royal Trust Co.   24
RUSSELL, Andy   *143-144*
RUTHERFORD, Alexander
  Cameron   *17-18*, 22
"Rutherford, Reliability and
  Railways"   18
Ryley, Alta.   115
Saddle Lake Indian Reserve
  164
Sarcee Indian Reserve   34, 67
SCARLETT, Earle Parkhill
  121-122
SCHOCTOR, Joseph H.
  160-161
School Foundation Program
  125
SCURFIELD, Ralph   116
SIFTON, A.L.; Premier   26
SIFTON, Victor   142
SIMPSON, Jimmy   *57-58*
Smith, Alta.   119
SMITH, Becky   167
SMITH, Graham   167
SMITH, William Donald
  166-167
SNOW, John   133
Society of Artists, Alberta   94
Son of Eli   115
SOUTHAM, Dorothy Jean
  126
Sowing Seeds in Danny   49
Sports Hall of Fame, Alberta
  114, 166, 167
Sports Hall of Fame, Edmon-
  ton   114
Spring Coulee, Alta.   30
St. Albert, Alta.   21
St. Paul, Alta.   22
Standard Oil   161

174

Standoff, Alta.   29
STEINHAUER, Ralph Garvin;
   Lt.-Gov.   *163-164*
STEPHANSON, Stephan G.
   30-32
Stoney Indians   58
Strathcona, Alta.   17, 18, 26,
   71
sugar beet industry   28
Sulphur Mountain, Alta.   93
Suncor Inc.   14
Swan Hills, Alta.   119
SWIFT, William Herbert
   124-125
Taber, Alta.   30, 87, 155
Tar Sands   51-52
Teachers' Assoc., Alberta   71
THOMPSON, D. Walter   69
THREE PERSONS, Tom
   28-30
Toronto *Globe*   18, 76
TORY, Henry Marshall   *22-23*,
   51
TransCanada Pipelines Limited
   162
TRELLE, Herman   *55-56*
TRUDEAU, Pierre Elliot;
   Prime Minister   152, 168
Turner Valley, Alta.   32, 126,
   133, 142
Ukrainian Professional and Busi-
   nessmen's Club   145
United Farmers of Alberta
   (UFA)   44, 45, 47, 50, 61,
   68, 88, 89, 92
Valleyview, Alta.   117
VANIER, Georges; Governor-
   General   148
Vanishing Point, The   128
Victoria Composite High
   School   53
VARLEY, F. H.   95

Vegreville, Alta.   144
Voix de la Solitude   78
Wabasca, Alta.   119
WARD, Maxwell William
   157-158
Wardair   157
WARE, John   14
Wasketanau, Alta.   155
Wembley, Alta.   56
Westcoast Transmission Ltd.
   134
Western Stock Growers Assoc.
   24
Wetaskiwin, Alta.   25-26, 69
Wetaskiwin Free Lance   25
Wheat Pool, Alberta   45
Whitecourt, Alta.   59
Whitefish Lake   164
Why Shoot the Teacher?   165
WILSON, Tom   58
WIEBE, Rudy   128
WISE WOOD, Henry   *44-45*
Women's Christian Temperance
   Union   49, 61
WOODSWORTH, James S.
   68
World Peace Foundation   163
Yellowhead, Alta.   46
Yellowknife Airways Limited
   157
Young Men's Christian Assoc.
   (YMCA)   122
Youville Residential School   21

References and Suggested Reading

Artibise, Alan, *Western Canada since 1870: A Select Bibliography*, Vancouver, 1978.

Berry, G.L., *The Whoop-Up Trail*, Edmonton, 1953.

Berton, Pierre, *The Last Spike*, Toronto, 1974.

Bezanson, A.M., *Sodbusters Invade the Peace*, New York, 1954.

Blue, John, *Alberta Past and Present*, Chicago, 1924.

Butler, W.F., *The Great Lone Land*, Edmonton, 1968.

Cashman, Tony, *An Illustrated History of Western Canada*, Edmonton, 1971.

Dempsey, Hugh A., *Crowfoot*, Edmonton, 1972; *Jerry Potts, Plainsman*, Calgary, 1966; *Men in Scarlet*, Toronto, 1974.

Edmonds, W.E., *Edmonton Past and Present*, Edmonton, 1943.

Erasmus, Peter, *Buffalo Days and Nights*, Calgary, 1976.

Fetherstonhaugh, R.C. *The Royal Canadian Mounted Police*, New York, 1938.

Hill, Douglas, *The Opening of the Canadian West*, Toronto, 1977

Howard, Joseph K., *Strange Empire*, Toronto, 1974.

Hughes, Katherine, *Father Lacombe*, Toronto, 1911.

Kaye, V.J., *Early Ukrainian Settlement in Canada*, Toronto, 1964.

MacEwan, Grant, *Between the Red and the Rockies*, Toronto, 1952.

MacGregor, James C., *A History of Alberta*, Edmonton, 1972.

Nute, Grace L., *The Voyageur*, Winnipeg, 1972.

Robertson, Heather, *Salt of the Earth*, Toronto, 1974.

Stanley, G.F.G., *The Birth of Western Canada*, Toronto, 1960.

Stegner, Wallace, *Wolf Willow*, New York, 1962.

Thomas, Lewis G., *The Prairie West to 1905; A Canadian Source Book*, Toronto, 1974.

Woodcock, George, *Canada and the Canadians*, Toronto, 1970.

Weibe, Rudy, *Alberta / A Celebration*, Edmonton, 1979.

29, 710